Dedicated

Steps of Faith in God's Plan

ALSO BY BRENDA PACE

Journey of a Military Wife

    Dedicated: Steps of Faith in God's Plan
    Devoted: Steps of Love Toward Healthy Relationships
    Deployed: Steps of Hope in Times of Uncertainty
    Directed: Steps of Peace in Times of Transition

Medals Above My Heart: The Rewards of Being a Military Wife
(Coauthored with Carol McGlothlin)

The One Year Yellow Ribbon Devotional: Take a Stand
in Prayer for Our Nation and Those Who Serve
(Coauthored with Carol McGlothlin)

Dedicated

Steps of Faith in God's Plan

BRENDA PACE

 AMERICAN BIBLE SOCIETY

Philadelphia

DEDICATED: STEPS OF FAITH IN GOD'S PLAN
(JOURNEY OF A MILITARY WIFE SERIES)

By Brenda Pace
Edited by Peter Edman, Davina McDonald, and Stacey Wright

© 2016 American Bible Society
All rights reserved.

ISBN 978-1-941448-57-1
ABS Item 124538

Design by Jordan Grove
Cover image by Joshua Wann

Set in Arno Pro and Avenir

American Bible Society
101 North Independence Mall East
Philadelphia, PA 19106

www.american.bible

Printed in the United States of America

Contents

An online version of JOURNEY OF A MILITARY WIFE is also available. You can find this book series, small group study guides, and a place to invite others to share this journey with you at www.MilitaryWife.bible.

Journey 1

Dedicated to God's Plan

Introduction

I had no idea what I was getting into when my husband raised his hand to take an oath for military service. He made a commitment to serve his country and I was committed to be his partner in life. After that oath, at least for a season, that commitment included military life. As a follower of Christ, I was dedicated to live my life for Christ wherever the road led—the detours and rough roads as well as the smooth, easy paths. Military life has certainly brought them all. My journey has been one of personal fulfillment, deep relationships, and spiritual transformation.

God is looking for women willing to take a step of faith and discover their place in his plan. The Armed Services Ministry at American Bible Society is committed to help you be a dedicated disciple of Christ. We invite you to take a series of thirty-day journeys of faith in the pages of the Bible. The journeys in this volume explore what it means to be a dedicated person, one who lives life with purpose and single-minded faithfulness. First, we will trace the steps toward a dedicated life through the journey of Abraham and Sarah in the book of Genesis.

Each day features a devotional waypoint. A *waypoint* is a stopping place on a journey. These waypoints may be places where you want to return, or they may be a point on a route or a significant landmark. Waypoints on this journey will help you focus prayerfully on a topic that can enhance your dedication to God and your understanding of God's purpose for you. Each day before you begin, pray this verse from Psalm 119:18: Lord, "*Open my eyes, that I may behold wondrous things out of your law.*"

Think about finding fellow sojourners and study God's Word together. As a companion to this book you will find online at MilitaryWife.Bible a set of Bible studies complete with leader and participant notes to guide your discussion.

Welcome to the journey!

Waypoint 1

The steps of a dedicated wife

Read

> So then, my friends, because of God's great mercy to us I appeal to you: Offer yourselves as a living sacrifice to God, dedicated to his service and pleasing to him. This is the true worship that you should offer. (Romans 12:1 GNT)

Reflect

We see *dedication* on display in loyalty, devotion, and commitment to a person or cause. As a military wife, the word "dedication" brings to my mind women like Martha Washington. General George's wife was one of many brave women who followed her husband to battlefield encampments to ease some of the hardships of war. History records women who tried to bring some of the comforts of home to the front lines by cooking, cleaning, and nursing the wounded. Some women even fired muskets right alongside their husbands.[1] That is what I call fierce dedication.

Today's military wife does not follow her husband to the combat zone, but she still shows her dedication by her willingness to continue the pioneer spirit of military wives long past. My modern-day list of dedicated military wives includes Susan, Cindy, Jennifer, Celeste, Holly, and countless others. These friends have endured multiple deployments and numerous moves, but they remain deeply dedicated to their husbands and the military communities in which they live and serve. They will tell you that their dedication to Christ translates into dedication to their husbands and subsequently to military life.

As a Christ-follower, I am dedicated to my husband because I love him and honor the marriage vows I made to him. Over time my dedication to him has grown deeper as the commitment we made is proven in daily life. I support his choice of career while I live into God's call on my own life. We will see through the journey of Abraham and Sarah that there is more to living a dedicated life than may readily be observed. Are you curious? Then let's keep moving! Where will your steps of dedication lead you today?

Respond

What are the areas of your life in which you display dedication? How would you prioritize those areas?

Prayer for the journey

Father, I want to be fully dedicated and committed to your purposes in the world. Help me see how being a dedicated military wife fits into that plan. I stand ready for the adventure. Amen.

Waypoint 2

An unlikely conversation

Read Genesis 12 to acquaint yourself with the beginning of Abraham and Sarah's journey.

Now the LORD said to Abram ... (Genesis 12:1a)

Reflect

The journey for Abraham and his family began with God initiating a relationship with him. Scripture does not give details, only the words, *"The LORD said to Abram ..."* (Genesis 12:1a). On the surface it seems natural for God to speak to someone important in the Bible. What makes this scene unnatural is the fact that, at this time, Abraham was *not* important. In fact, from all indications he was not even following God. The Old Testament book of Joshua tells us that Abraham's father was an idol worshipper (Joshua 24:2). Picture Abraham as a man who lived in a pagan, idol-worshipping world, being addressed by the creator God of the universe!

God called Abraham because he had great plans for him. He was not singled out because he had a godly heritage, was in the right family, or grew up in the right church. God initiated a conversation with Abraham that interrupted his life and changed the course of his journey. God put him on a track that would ultimately lead to a new path of redemption for the world through Christ.

Where are you on your spiritual journey? You may have little to no awareness or concern for spiritual things. You may have a desire to know more about a life dedicated to God. You may be a dedicated follower of Christ. Just like God had great plans for Abraham, God has great plans for you. Wherever you are in the journey, he wants to take you to the next step. The journey for Abraham led him out of a life of purposeless service of idols and into a life of purposeful faith in God. Where will your journey take you? What conversation is the God of the universe initiating with you that may lead to redemption or transformation in some area of your life?

Respond

Have you ever had a conversation with another person that changed the course of your thinking about something? Has God's call changed your life? How?

Prayer for the journey

Father, thank you for initiating a relationship with me that will set me on a path of new life in Christ. Help me honor you as I live out my purpose today. Amen.

Waypoint 3

Orientation tour

> The LORD said to Abram, "Leave your country, your relatives, and your father's home, and go to a land that I am going to show you." (Genesis 12:1 GNT)

The sign read: "Guided tour to the places that matter to you!"

The advertisement was for the Orientation Tour at our latest duty station. I was not keen on being herded on and off a bus, but I was tired of getting lost. I needed someone to show me. As hard as it was for me, I signed up. I got on the bus, and you know what? The tour was a pleasant surprise. I not only learned physical locations of places, but I discovered great resources my new community had to offer. An added bonus was meeting some other newcomers.

The promise of God to Abraham in Genesis 12:1 was for him to go to "a land that I am going to show you." Sounds like an Orientation Tour to me. Yet I cannot compare the tour Abraham signed up for and the tour I took. I had a good idea of the stops along the way. Abraham knew nothing. God asked Abraham to "get on the bus" and trust that God would show him the places he was to go. Sisters, dedication is joining God's tour before you know where it is going or what you will experience.

The New Testament book of Hebrews describes Abraham as a man who lived by faith. Abraham could tell you specifically what he left behind to follow God's call, but what was ahead was a big question mark. The call for each of us to follow God is not a call to trust in a plan, but to trust a person. God would show him places along the way, but as we saw in our first journey, Abraham's Orientation Tour was not so much about geography as it was about relationship.

Abraham had a willingness to go where God would lead. God had much to show Abraham. He has much to show you. Are you willing to take his tour?

Respond

"Dedication is joining God's tour before you know where it is going or what you will experience." What thoughts come to mind when you read this phrase? What is your usual reaction when you are asked to go to a place about which you know nothing? What does Hebrews 11:9–10 have to say about Abraham's true destination?

Prayer for the journey

Lord, help me grow in grace as I walk with you. Teach me to trust you even when I cannot see where you lead. Amen.

Waypoint 4

Be all you can be

Read

> Now the LORD said to Abram, "Go from your country and your kindred and your father's house to the land that I will show you. And I will make of you a great nation, and I will bless you and make your name great, so that you will be a blessing." (Genesis 12:1–2)

Reflect

The recruiting slogan for the Army in 1981 was "Be all you can be!" The jingle was a successful attention-grabber. The promise for a young person to reach their full potential encouraged many to find a military recruiter and sign over a few years of life to Uncle Sam and his friend the Drill Sergeant.

Likely, no recruiter enlisted you as a military wife. But the promise of that slogan is one you can take as your own, if you are willing.

Willingness is an inclination or readiness to do something, and it is a trait displayed in the life of Abraham and his wife Sarah.² God invited Abraham to follow him into an unknown territory with the promise of making him all he could be. Sarah's willingness to go on the journey is impressive. Travel in the Near East during this time was dangerous and difficult. The road system was—well, there was no road system. The journey was by foot, with a donkey to serve as the moving van. Sarah had no military sponsor to write and give her information about what to expect at her next duty station.

Besides the logistical challenges, Abraham and Sarah were not young people. If the setting were today, Sarah would be looking for a place to put down roots. Yet she was willing to follow her husband into the unknown.

Military life can be an adventure into the unknown. You may have left home, family, and friends to follow your husband to an unfamiliar place. The adventure is not without challenge, but it makes for an interesting life. The happiest military wives are those who have—or can cultivate—a willingness to embrace the unknown. Are you willing to do all you can do in order to be all you can be? The good news is that God promises to be with you. We will see that his promises to Abraham and Sarah were fulfilled—and that his promises to you are sure.

Respond

Do you struggle with having a willing heart when it comes to being a military wife? List your specific struggles in a journal. Make this list a prayer guide.

Prayer for the journey

Father, please give me a willing heart to follow you. Help me to trust that your promises are true and that you want to use my experience as a military wife to make me into the best follower I can be. Amen.

Waypoint 5
A trail of blessing

Read

"I will bless those who bless you, and him who dishonors you I will curse, and in you all the families of the earth shall be blessed." (Genesis 12:3)

Reflect

Up until this point in Genesis there is mention of blessing, but there is more mention of events that are opposite to blessing. Remember Adam and Eve and their quick exit from the perfect garden? What about Noah and the flood or the devastating results of the Tower of Babel? The biblical story takes a turn in Genesis 12 when God interrupts the life of Abraham and declares that all people on earth will be blessed through him.

That word *blessing* gets thrown around a lot, but what does it really mean? If I hear someone sneeze, I usually respond with, "God bless you!" I often use the word *Blessings* as the closing to a note or letter. My husband and I pray a blessing over our meals before we eat. I know how being blessed feels when I gaze at a recent photo of my family. Yet, this is not an adequate definition of blessing. Blessing is more than something I say, or something I feel. Indeed, the blessing described in Genesis 12:3 is more than words and emotions.

In general terms, God's blessings include his favor, protection, and care.[3] The word *bless* in Genesis 12:3 conveys spiritual and physical enrichment. In the case of Abraham, God physically blessed him with land, crops, and livestock that would also benefit other families who lived in close proximity. However, the word in context places more emphasis on the spiritual blessing that God has in mind, the way that *"all the families of the earth"* would learn about the one true God through Abraham's relationship with him.[4] God was going to give Abraham great promises, while at the same time he envisioned Abraham looking beyond himself to share promises and hope with others.

As a military wife you can enjoy the blessings that come from your husband's military service by way of such things as support groups, medical care, and a sense of job security. The greatest blessing comes as you become involved in your community and leave a trail of blessing in the lives of others. How will you do that today?

Respond

List in your journal some ways you have been blessed by military life. What are some ways you have blessed others?

Prayer for the journey

Lord, enable me to view my life through the lens of blessing. Remind me of the blessings that are mine and use me to bless others. Amen.

Waypoint 6
The first step is the hardest

> So Abram went, as the LORD had told him, and Lot
> went with him. Abram was seventy-five years old when
> he departed from Haran. (Genesis 12:4)

Abraham was born in a city called Ur, a place located in the
south of what we now know as Iraq—yes, that Iraq. Heard of it?
Scholars tell us that Ur was a thriving city filled with educational,
cultural, and economic opportunities. Abraham's father Terah
then moved the family north and west to the city of Haran
(Genesis 11:31). When his father died, God directed Abraham to
leave Haran and go to Canaan (see also Acts 7:4). The call God
gave to Abraham was blunt. He used two action words military
families know well: leave and go.

At face value this directive does not seem such a challenge,
but when you look at the culture of the Near East, you see this
challenge was more than meets the eye. In Abraham's day to
leave your family was to leave your significance and security. God
asked Abraham and his wife Sarah to leave behind their country,
their nationality, their clan, and ultimately their identity.[5]

Maybe you can relate to this story. Perhaps you lived in a
city you enjoyed, surrounded by family and friends. One day an
official document headlined ORDERS arrived with the *order* to
leave and *go* to an unfamiliar place. No journey can commence
without a first step, and my guess is the first step out of Haran
was a hard one for Abraham and Sarah, just as it may have been
for you.

My friend Kay recalls the day her husband entered military service. She had been born and reared in the same small town where her family had deep roots. The idea of living anywhere else was unthinkable, yet that is what she did as a military wife. When asked about what made leaving her hometown so difficult she said, "I was afraid of the unknown. I didn't know who I was outside my homogeneous bubble." If you talk to Kay today she will tell you the first step was the hardest, but she would do it all over again in a heartbeat: "The journey has been amazing! I thought I would lose my identity when I left home. Instead, God has used military life to grow me into who he called me to be. Don't get me wrong, I love my hometown, but God had a plan that included me taking a step into unknown territory. Yes, the first step was the hardest, but he's been with me each step of the way."

Respond

Is God asking you to take a step of faith in some area? What keeps you from taking the first step?

Prayer for the journey

Lord, give me courage to take the first step
- to leave the familiar
- to meet a new neighbor
- to get involved in a ministry
- to forgive a friend
- to make a wise choice.

Help me step out in your name and in your power. Amen.

Waypoint 7
They set out

> And Abram took Sarai his wife, and Lot his brother's son, and all their possessions that they had gathered, and the people that they had acquired in Haran and they set out to go to the land of Canaan. (Genesis 12:5a)

Reflect

"She set her sights on the goal."
"She was set up for success."
"Her heart is set on it."

The use of the word *set* in these statements creates a context of determination and focus, doesn't it? The mood of Genesis 12:5 would be different if it read: "They began their journey toward the land of Canaan." Abraham did not just start the journey—he *set out!*

Someone who *sets out* has a goal in mind and will make an earnest attempt to accomplish that goal. Abraham and his household set out with purpose to see the Promised Land. They set out determined that they would not get distracted and would reach their destination.

The journey no doubt brought emotional upheaval, but it also brought physical challenge. The expedition from Haran to Canaan was about five hundred miles. The paths were rough and the pace was slow. Imagine hiking the Appalachian Trail with your kids and all your belongings for five hundred miles. I don't know about you, but my *set out* would quickly turn to *sit down!*

Abraham had to see the goal of God's promise in his mind to be able to make such a trek. That is the way of any goal, isn't it? We have to own it. We have to set our minds on achievement in order to accomplish the goal.

Have you ever thought about goals as they relate to military life? In other words, what kind of military wife have you *set out* to become? I encourage you today not to view military life as a temporary state of existence, but to set goals for this season of your life. Whether short term goals for your current duty station, or long term goals for the time of your husband's military obligation, there are important questions you can ask yourself to bring focus and determination to your journey.

Respond

Ask yourself:
- How do I want to grow as a person?
- Where do I want to be in my relationships?
- What do I want my finances to look like?
- Is this a place to continue my education?
- Are there opportunities for Christian service?
- Are there opportunities for leadership training?
- How do I want to grow in my faith and relationship to God?

Prayer for the journey

Father, I *set out* today with determination and focus. Help me set goals that are pleasing to the direction you want my life to go, and then equip me to live today with purpose. Amen.

Waypoint 8

This is not what I expected!

> At that time the Canaanites were in the land.
> (Genesis 12:6b)

Reflect

"Make sure you're covered and run straight for the light!"

This is not a statement from a science fiction novel or action thriller. The words do not refer to dodging bullets or a near-death experience. This is what my husband said to me while working at a summer camp in Minnesota. What was he instructing me to run from, you ask? Mosquitoes! No, the mosquito is not the Minnesota state bird, as many quip, but it is the state pest!

The invitation to speak at a summer camp by the lake brought expectations of a paid vacation in a lovely woodland setting. My husband was the guest speaker and I was going along to enjoy nature at its best. Or so I thought. My expectation of an idyllic vacation was crushed as I battled the tiny, but extremely annoying, mosquito.

One life lesson from that summer camp is that no matter how idyllic your circumstances, there will be difficulties. Even when you are in the right place, at the right time, doing the right thing, challenges will be present. Abraham was at the place the Lord sent him, at the time the Lord sent him; yet he was faced with the problem of Canaanites living in the land God said would be his. I will give you a hint of what is to come: The Canaanites were going to prove a much greater threat than an army of mosquitoes. They were downright anti-neighborly.[6]

The truth is, sometimes the things God asks of us do not come in a simple and direct manner.[7] In a perfect world there are no mosquitoes or Canaanites, but we do not live in a perfect world. In the real world your dedication as a military wife will be tested by situations—and people. The tests may come by way of an annoying neighbor, an uncooperative military support group, or a command climate that makes your husband's work unpleasant.

Hope can be found in the words of Psalm 46:1: "God is our shelter and strength, always ready to help in times of trouble." The expectation of his help will never be disappointed.

Respond

Think of a time when you felt you were at the right place, at the right time. Were your expectations met or were there unforeseen annoyances? How did you handle any disappointment?

Prayer for the journey

Lord, I can get bent out of shape over the smallest annoyance. Help me look at any obstacle as an opportunity for your grace to work in and through me. Help me rejoice in hope, be patient in tribulation, and stay constant in prayer. Amen.

Waypoint 9

The area code of faith

> Then the LORD appeared to Abram and said, "To your offspring I will give this land." So he built there an altar to the LORD, who had appeared to him. From there he moved to the hill country on the east of Bethel and pitched his tent, with Bethel on the west and Ai on the east. And there he built an altar to the LORD and called upon the name of the LORD. And Abram journeyed on, still going toward the Negeb. (Genesis 12:7–9)

Reflect

You know you're a military wife when ... your driver's license, car registration, phone area code, and zip code are each from a different state.

There was a time when that description fit me. All the official necessities are now correctly registered in the state in which I reside. My cell phone number, however, remains the same. I have long since left the 910 area code, but I have kept that number. Why? Because it is symbolic of a place where my faith grew exponentially.

In that area code I called out to God ...

... when I was lonely and he reminded me of his presence.

... when I was afraid and he reminded me of his protection.

... when I was discouraged and he reminded me of his hope.

... when I was vulnerable and he reminded me of his help.

... when I was anxious and he reminded me of his peace.

... when I was weak and he reminded me of his strength.

In that area code God strengthened me for the journey ahead. I left that place stronger in my faith and more confident of my eternal purpose. I do not plan to change my cell phone number because its area code is a spiritual landmark. Without a doubt an area code is an unusual landmark of faith, but a landmark can be anything that brings to remembrance an aspect of spiritual history and formation.

Shechem and Bethel became landmarks of faith for Abraham. God shared a few more details with him at Shechem about the promise to make his name great. In response, Abraham built an altar in confirmation of and silent thanksgiving for the promise of God.[8]

Respond

Do you have places that you consider landmarks of your faith in God? Abraham honored God with the physical act of building an altar. What are ways that you honor God?

Prayer for the journey

Lord, make me aware of your presence today. Open my eyes to see your glory in the people and places I encounter and strengthen my faith with each step. Amen.

Waypoint 10

When faith takes a detour

Read

> Now there was a famine in the land. So Abram went down to Egypt to sojourn there, for the famine was severe in the land. (Genesis 12:10)

Reflect

"I feel alone. This house is no companion. My children are uncommunicative. My husband is too tired to talk when he finally gets home. Everything takes too much effort. Why did we have to move here? I tell myself this was the right direction for our family but today I'm not sure. God, do you even care?"

I'm not proud to admit this ranting came from my journal. This was my husband's dream assignment. We purchased our first home in a community that had high ratings for quality of life. Yet the promise that led us to this place faded as the challenges of real life arose. In a symbolic sense there was famine in the land.

On the heels of God's appearance to Abraham, he walks right into a famine. God did not say anything about a famine. He spoke of promise—land—children—a great name—not a famine! Perhaps Abraham questioned if he heard God at all.

What did Abraham do in the face of this obstacle? He took a detour from God's itinerary. Egypt was not on the route, but famine was not on the agenda. He had to do something to feed his family, didn't he? Or did he? Doesn't this detour to Egypt argue against God's care for Abraham promised in the blessing?[9] Was God really able to care for him in this new land?[10]

Doubts and questions are common when obstacles appear. We face the same challenge today that Abraham faced: Will we allow God to use obstacles to grow our faith? Abraham took his eyes off the God of the promise and focused on the threat to the promise.

If Abraham and his family, who held an exceptional place in God's plan, encountered challenges, we should approach our Christian life with the expectation that we will face challenges too. There are times we struggle to hear God's voice and question the direction we are sure he told us to take. When we decide to take matters into our own hands, even then, we can rest assured that the Lord can turn us in the right direction.

Respond

Are you struggling with an obstacle that seems to keep you from growing in your relationship with God? Write it down in your journal. If you can't put it in words yet, ask God to show it to you more clearly.

Prayer for the journey

Lord, help me to trust you when obstacles seem to block your will for my life. Strengthen my trust that you care for me and will provide for every need. Amen.

Waypoint 11

In a moment of panic!

> When he was about to enter Egypt, he said to Sarai his wife, "I know that you are a woman beautiful in appearance, and when the Egyptians see you, they will say, 'This is his wife.' Then they will kill me, but they will let you live. Say you are my sister, that it may go well with me because of you, and that my life may be spared for your sake." (Genesis 12:11–13)

Reflect

Am I the only one who has endured the humiliation of going to a military social event only to forget the name of someone important (like the commander's wife)? Am I the only one who has stretched the truth (just a little bit) to save face and protect myself? Am I the only one who has panicked in a stressful situation and made a foolish decision?

I read Genesis 12:11–13 and say, "Whew! I'm not the only one!" Abraham, a man who became the patriarch of Israel, a friend of God, and a hero of faith, did all of these things.

Up until this time Abraham is pictured doing what God asked him to do. The Abraham portrayed in Genesis 12:1–10 seems to be calm and obedient, but the unexpected news of famine transforms this picture from calmness to anxiety.[11] In fact, the first words reported from his mouth are words to encourage his wife to lie. Excuse me?

Before my criticism seems too harsh, I note that Abraham did not deny God, he simply forgot him.[12] He was new to this "walking with God" thing and in a panic he turned to his own devices. At this point in his life this was his default, but—looking ahead—we will see how the default of panic was transformed to a default of trust.

In a moment of perceived powerlessness, Abraham made some poor decisions. Why? He was a man in process. His growing faith was tested and he failed the test. I find comfort in this tale of disappointment. You see, Abraham's failure did not stop God from growing him into a mighty person of faith. Similarly, the mistakes you and I make will not keep God from growing us into the people he calls us to be. Because of Jesus, there is forgiveness when we sin and help when we panic. Our default can be one of trust as we keep our focus on God.

Respond
Is anything causing you to feel panic in your soul today? Spend some time in prayer asking God to send you his peace.

Prayer for the journey
May I always be aware, Lord, of your presence. You are near, and nothing can shake me. Amen (from Psalm 16:8).

Waypoint 12
The law of attraction

> When Abram entered Egypt, the Egyptians saw that
> the woman was very beautiful. And when the princes
> of Pharaoh saw her, they praised her to Pharaoh.
> And the woman was taken into Pharaoh's house.
> (Genesis 12:14–15)

Reflect

She had just moved to a new town. She was lonely. Her husband was busy at his new job. He was consumed with making a good first impression. She felt invisible. She felt marginalized. She felt vulnerable. A lingering look and a little attention from a stranger was all it took for marital dedication to be put to the test.

Can we say right up front that the dedication of Sarah to Abraham in Genesis 12:14–15 is above and beyond? Just for today, let's not focus on Abraham's outlandish request and the selfish motivation that landed her in Pharaoh's harem and just focus on Sarah. Beautiful Sarah found herself in a precarious situation not unlike the subject of the scenario above.

In today's supermodel world, it is hard for us to wrap our minds around a woman in her mid-sixties being considered such a beauty. While Sarah's move into Pharaoh's harem was caused by Abraham's fears for self-preservation, there's a warning here for women. The warning is to be on guard during those times when you feel vulnerable. Be watchful during those times you feel less than attractive. Be careful during those times when your reality does not match your fantasy.

We can only speculate whether Sarah was flattered by the attraction she received from Pharaoh and his court. We can only speculate whether Sarah, if given a choice, would have been tempted to stay in Pharaoh's household. Think about it: wandering in the desert and living in a tent versus being told you are beautiful and living in a palace. Temptation sounds pretty credible in that situation.

You can only speculate what you might do when someone other than your husband finds you attractive. Don't laugh. It happens. Is it inevitable? No. Is it possible? Yes. Marital faithfulness is the responsibility of both husband and wife. Military wives are often faced with extended times of absence from their husbands. You may be incredulous at the thought of marital infidelity, but Scripture wisely tells us to be on our guard. *"If you think you are standing firm you had better be careful that you do not fall"* (1 Corinthians 10:12).

Respond

How can you be proactive in protecting your marriage? Have you and your husband ever attended a marriage conference or taken a class that focuses on God's design for marriage? What can you do today to strengthen your marriage?

Prayer for the journey

Bless my marriage, Lord, with your peace. Help us to be kind, considerate, and concerned for one another. Increase the faith my husband and I have in you. Amen.

Waypoint 13

Because of her

And for her sake he dealt well with Abram ...
(Genesis 12:16a)

Reflect

What an encouraging story of God's concern for Sarah.[13]
Consider that for her sake Pharaoh dealt well with Abraham to
the point of giving him expensive gifts. There is no indication
that Sarah was affected by the plague that assaulted Pharaoh's
household. Even after Pharaoh realized his association with Sarah
had caused his affliction, it would have been understandable to
order Abraham to return all the gifts, send him to prison, or
decree a death sentence. Instead, he sent Abraham on his way
along with Sarah and "everything he owned." We have no clue
of Sarah's feelings but we see God's actions, caring for her as he
protected her and returned her to her husband.

This kindness of God reminds me of a time God showed his
care for me. My husband gave me a lovely ring for an anniversary.
I had not had the ring long when I was volunteering at a gift shop
sponsored by the Wives Club in Korea. I spent the day packing
and unpacking boxes, checking merchandise for customers, and
bagging purchases that were carried out the door to destinations
near and far. At some point, I reached down to touch my new
ring. My hand instinctively jerked upward as I discovered one of
the diamonds was missing. I sadly retraced my steps, resigned to
the fact that the stone was lost forever.

Later that day I opened my wallet to pay for a purchase. I
could not believe what I saw. There among the coins was a

beautiful little diamond. That stone could not have fallen out of its setting in a more protected place than my snapped-shut wallet.

The timing was not lost on me. Our family had just moved to Korea and I felt like that stone, as if I had fallen out of my setting. God showed me that day that I was precious to him. In his time, I would find the setting he prepared for me in this new place. It was enough for now to know he had not forgotten me.

God protected Sarah because she was an integral part of the promise he made to Abraham. Her setting in the plan was sure and God would bring it to pass in time.

There's a place in his plan for you too. His care for you is certain and his love for you is undeniable.

Respond
Do you ever question God's plan for you? What are some ways God has shown his care?

Prayer for the journey
Lord, forgive me when I doubt your care for me. Help me to remember that nothing can separate me from your love. Amen.

Waypoint 14

You win or lose by the way you choose

Read Genesis 13:1–13

> Then Abram said to Lot ... "Is not the whole land before you? Separate yourself from me. If you take the left hand, then I will go to the right, or if you take the right hand, then I will go to the left." And Lot lifted up his eyes and saw that the Jordan Valley was well watered everywhere like the garden of the LORD ... So Lot chose for himself all the Jordan Valley ... (Genesis 13:8–11)

Reflect

"If you can't say something nice, don't say anything at all." "If one of your friends jumped off a bridge, would you jump too?" "My goal is for you to become a productive member of society!"

In our home these phrases became family expressions meant to motivate our children. Truth be told, the statements brought more rolling of the eyes than motivation. From the time the children were toddlers, another common household phrase was: "You win or lose by the way you choose." Of all our family expressions, I hope this is the one passed to the next generation. Making wise choices is paramount to a good and godly life.

At this point in the journey, Abraham and his nephew Lot had become wealthy men. As they settled back at Bethel in Canaan again, they found that there was not enough room for them both.[14] There was not enough water and pasture land there for all the livestock they had accumulated, and Abraham's people and Lot's people began to quarrel. Someone had to go.

Abraham took the high road by giving Lot the option to take the land he wanted. The anxious and self-preserving Abraham who fled to Egypt in a panic is not the Abraham pictured in this scene. Here we see a calm and generous figure who chooses to renounce his option as the leader and elder and give his nephew first choice of the land.[15]

So Lot chooses, based on the beautiful land he sees.[16] His choice does not make me a fan of Lot. Then I consider my own history of "poor, self-centered, hide-the-biggest piece, take-the-best-place, and sneak-the-extra-portion" choices—and Lot starts sounding more like a kindred spirit!

A choice may not seem important at the time it is made, but it can set the course for life.[17]

Respond

What are some things to take into account that will help you make wise choices?

Prayer for the journey

Lord, give me a heart of wisdom, a heart that is willing to obey you. Help me to make wise choices. Amen.

Waypoint 15

Walking and praying

The Lord said to Abram, after Lot had separated from him, "Lift up your eyes and look from the place where you are, northward and southward and eastward and westward, for all the land that you see I will give to you and to your offspring forever. I will make your offspring as the dust of the earth, so that if one can count the dust of the earth, your offspring also can be counted. Arise, walk through the length and the breadth of the land, for I will give it to you." So Abram moved his tent and came and settled by the oaks of Mamre, which are at Hebron, and there he built an altar to the Lord. (Genesis 13:14–18)

Reflect

I met Ruth when our husbands attended a military school together. We were acquaintances who were happy for the possibility to become friends when we heard the news that both our families would be moving to Fort Benning, Georgia. In the providence of God we became neighbors on the same street.

Ruth and I walked in the evenings around the neighborhood for exercise and conversation. As we walked, we shared our frustrations about our new community, our fears about our husbands' new jobs, our concerns about our children's education, and our struggle to find our own places of ministry and service. Eventually, our walking and talking became walking and praying. Over time something interesting happened. As we walked and prayed for our neighbors, the neighborhood became something we cared about. As we walked and prayed for the school, the school became a place we cared about. As we walked and prayed for our husbands' jobs, the soldiers and their mission became something about which we cared.

God's instruction to Abraham to "walk through the length and the breadth of the land" that God promised to give him reminds me of the walks I took with my friend. While we walked and prayed the Lord made that place home for us. In Old Testament times, measuring out the land on foot was part of the action of taking possession of the land.[18] The promise of God to give the land to Abraham and his offspring was confirmed and sealed in Abraham as he obeyed and walked. An added benefit of walking with my friend is that our relationship grew strong. We remain the dearest of friends to this day. Abraham's relationship with God grew stronger as well with every step they took together.

Respond

Do you have a friend with whom you pray? If not, consider making it a priority to find someone to join you in praying for the needs of your community.

Prayer for the journey

Lord, I ask you to bless my military community. Strengthen relationships and bring harmony to each home. Amen.

Waypoint 16

In need of rescue

Read Genesis 14:11–16

> So the enemy took all the possessions of Sodom and
> Gomorrah, and all their provisions, and went their way.
> They also took Lot, the son of Abram's brother, who
> was dwelling in Sodom, and his possessions, and went
> their way. (Genesis 14:11–12)

Reflect

"The military is like a big family!" said a new military wife to me
after her husband's first few months on active duty service. My
response to her was a resounding, "Yes, it is!"

I did not know what it was like to live in community until
I became a military wife. I remember looking out my window
at one assignment to see dozens of children playing in our
backyard. The neighbors followed an unwritten code to watch
out for each other, especially when it came to the children. The
result of living so close was an awareness of needs. At times that
was a little uncomfortable, but it was more about helping than
getting in each other's business. The blessings outweighed the
frustrations. If I was ever in a jam, they came to my rescue.

Abraham's nephew Lot found himself in a jam. The choice
he made to take the best land for himself led to consequences
that put him in danger. Can't you see Abraham shaking his
head in frustration over Lot's predicament? I would not blame
Abraham if he had said, "He got himself in this mess and he can
get himself out." But instead he gathered his troops and went out
to rescue him.

Lot's situation was an extreme case, but the dedication Abraham displayed towards him is not unlike a military wife who has the opportunity to help others in her community. Jesus commands us to love others as he loved us (John 15:12–13). Each of us has an occasion to show Christ's love every day.

Respond

Look around your sphere of influence. Does anyone need rescue? Is there someone who might need to be rescued from loneliness? Invite her for coffee. Is there a young mom who might need to be rescued from isolation? Offer to babysit one afternoon. Is there a new military wife in the neighborhood who needs a rescue from unrealistic expectations? Take her on a tour of your favorite places in town and affirm her strengths.

Prayer for the journey

Make me an instrument of your peace today, Lord. Help me see the needs of others and take action to help. Amen.

Waypoint 17

An unexpected testimony

> After his return from the defeat of Chedorlaomer and the kings who were with him, the king of Sodom went out to meet him at the Valley of Shaveh (that is, the King's Valley). And Melchizedek king of Salem brought out bread and wine. (He was priest of God Most High.) And he blessed him and said, "Blessed be Abram by God Most High, Possessor of heaven and earth; and blessed be God Most High, who has delivered your enemies into your hand!" And Abram gave him a tenth of everything. (Genesis 14:17–20)

Reflect

Abraham found himself in what amounts to an international incident. Words like insurgency, revolt, conquest, and raid can all be used to describe the situation here in Genesis 14. Without going into details about the battle, we see that with 318 men Abraham successfully attacked and defeated his enemies. That makes it sound like Abraham brought about the defeat. But the hero was not Abraham—the hero was God. God's role in the victory was confirmed through an unexpected source.

After the battle, Melchizedek, king and priest of the city of Salem, met Abraham with a victory meal. His blessing and declaration of the Most High God's victory (v. 19–20) is not something we today would expect from a Canaanite king.

I did not know what to expect when my husband became a soldier. I grew up in a sheltered environment. I had no context of where God fit into military life. I certainly did not expect to find the finest Christian people I have ever had the privilege to know. Not having had any exposure to churches other than my own, I was pleasantly surprised to find so many military families who testified to the greatness of God.

Respond
When have you heard or received an unexpected blessing? How can you be an unexpected messenger of encouragement to someone as Melchizedek was to Abraham?

Prayer for the journey
Father, keep me faithful in serving you. Fill my heart with your love and use me to share that love with others today. Amen.

Waypoint 18
Selfless service

> And the king of Sodom said to Abram, "Give me the persons, but take the goods for yourself." But Abram said to the king of Sodom, "I have lifted my hand to the LORD, God Most High, Possessor of heaven and earth, that I would not take a thread or a sandal strap or anything that is yours, lest you should say, 'I have made Abram rich.' I will take nothing but what the young men have eaten, and the share of the men who went with me." (Genesis 14:21–24a)

Reflect

Selfless service is a term that conjures dramatic rescues in the face of life-threatening danger. Dramatic rescues and life-threatening danger, however, are not everyday occurrences. What part can selfless service play in everyday life?

I read a story in 2013 about a young Army specialist's wife who inadvertently became the leader of her Family Readiness Group (FRG) when the commander's wife was not interested in the job. The young woman worked hard to make the FRG a support for other military spouses in the unit. The challenge came when a new commander came in—and his wife *was* interested in leading the FRG. Great potential for drama!

The new commander's wife could have strong-armed her way into what was rightfully her position. Instead, she met with the young FRG leader and got to know her. The article affirmed both women for their selfless service as they worked together to put the needs of soldiers and their families above all else. They were willing to listen to each other rather than compete for position. The young wife remained the leader of the group and the commander's wife became the adviser. The new commander stated, "Both women should be commended for the humility they demonstrated in handling a delicate situation. They put the needs of soldiers and their families above all else."[19]

Selfless service is an act performed without any expectation of reward. It is the type of service that Abraham exhibited following the victorious battle in Genesis 14. The king of Sodom offered Abraham a portion of the spoils of war. Abraham had every right to take the plunder, but he chose not to accept the offer in order to remain above reproach in the eyes of his Canaanite neighbors. He surrendered his rights and refused personal gain in order to keep God's name untarnished.

Respond

What is your motivation for service? Would you continue to serve in an area even if you were not recognized?

Prayer for the journey

Lord, I want to live a life that points others to you. Help me never tarnish your name by my words, attitudes, or actions. Amen.

Waypoint 19

Dedicated to a promise

Read Genesis 15:1–6

> After these things the word of the LORD came to Abram in a vision: "Fear not, Abram, I am your shield; your reward shall be very great." (Genesis 15:1)

Reflect

Aren't you impressed when you see a chest full of ribbons or medals on someone in the military? Each has a story. Each represents a mission. Some medals represent completion of time in a job while others represent hazardous duty or exemplary service.

We occasionally read about people who display ribbons they did not earn. In an effort to appear more brave, accomplished, or advanced they may purchase ribbons at the Clothing Sales Store. Such ribbons count for nothing. Only medals presented by a legitimate leader count as a true reward.

Call me crazy, but Genesis 15 reminds me of a military ribbon ceremony. Think about it: Abraham has just fought a successful military campaign and he stands before his Commander, who tells him, "I will give you a great reward." Abraham's reward was not for leading a victorious battle, because God was the one who brought the victory. The reward was for his faith.

The only reward that would mean anything to him, though, would be a son—and that was impossible at his age. Abraham questioned God. He reasoned that the reward of an heir would have to come through one of his servants, which in his mind was like going to the Clothing Sales Store and buying one of those fake ribbons for his chest. I don't blame Abraham for such thoughts. Wouldn't you question the idea of becoming a first-time father if you were beyond the age of a grandpa?

God did not place any stars of award on Abraham's chest or shoulders, but he told him to go look up at the sky and try to count the stars. Abraham's reward would be that great and it was going to start with his son—his very own "born-in-his-old-age" son. Do you know what Abraham did when God said this to him? He believed. *He believed.* His journey had brought him to a place where he trusted what God said. He believed it even if he did not see it.

Respond

Recall a time when you had doubts about God's plan for your life. How did you respond? Do you have doubts about God's plan now? As you learn about Abraham and see his faith develop, how might that develop your faith?

Prayer for the journey

Lord, you revealed more of yourself to Abraham in the midst of his doubts. Help me to believe you are at work in my life, even when I do not see you. Amen.

Waypoint 20
When it's hard to wait

> Now Sarai, Abram's wife, had borne him no children. She had a female Egyptian servant whose name was Hagar. And Sarai said to Abram, "Behold now, the LORD has prevented me from bearing children. Go in to my servant; it may be that I shall obtain children by her. And Abram listened to the voice of Sarai. So after Abram had lived ten years in the land of Canaan, Sarai, Abram's wife, took Hagar and gave her to Abram her husband as a wife. (Genesis 16:1–3)

True confession: I can be impatient. I do not have to think hard for examples. There is the time I drove 45 MPH in a 25 MPH zone and had to endure the humiliation of military police traffic school. (Does a car even register the 15–25 MPH speeds posted on military installations?) And I cannot count the many outfits I could not wait to buy, only to find them 50–75 percent off the next week. Impatience has cost me both time and money.

Waiting is hard. In the case of Abraham and Sarah, a decade passed after God promised an heir. Who could blame Sarah for taking matters into her own hands? God said there would be a child and Sarah's biological clock had stopped ticking. Surely God needed a little help.

Before we get too critical of Sarah, it is useful to know that the customs of the day allowed for surrogate motherhood if there was an infertile wife. Survival of an agrarian family depended on sons to carry on the work. It may have been an accepted practice, but was it part of God's plan? Sarah was Abraham's wife. She and Abraham were one flesh. The promised son was to come from her.[20]

God's timing frequently requires waiting. Getting ahead of his plan has consequences that become evident as the scene in Genesis 16 plays out. Sarah's impatience resulted in a loss of respect and confidence. She lost confidence in Abraham's dedication to her, Hagar lost job security, and Abraham almost lost the son Hagar bore him.

Opportunities to learn to wait are built into military life, from the simple act of going to the commissary on payday to the emotional experience of deployment. Take advantage of such opportunities to cultivate a life of waiting well, and allow God to sustain you in the process.

Respond

How has military life helped you learn patience? Are you prone to wait patiently on God or take matters into your own hands?

Prayer for the journey

Lord, I often find it hard to wait. It's easy to get ahead of your plan. Deepen my trust in you during times when I long for what can only come in your time. Amen.

Waypoint 21

The God who sees me

Read Genesis 16:4–15

> The angel of the LORD found her by a spring of water in the wilderness, the spring on the way to Shur. And he said, "Hagar, servant of Sarai, where have you come from and where are you going?" (Genesis 16:7–8a)

> So she called the name of the LORD who spoke to her, "You are a God of seeing," for she said, "Truly here I have seen him who looks after me." (Genesis 16:13)

Reflect

"Magic Mirror, tell me today, have all my friends had fun at play? I see Jana and Cathy, Karen and Tabitha. I see Billy and Gregory, Joseph and Ben." Six-year-old me listened intently with the hope that my name would be called as Miss Marsha looked into her Magic Mirror. I watched *Romper Room* religiously, convinced that the perky TV host saw me on those rare times she called my name.

As a military wife my name and personal information sometimes do not seem very important. "Dependent" is the designation assigned to me on lists and official documents. I know my husband's Social Security number, but often forget my own.

Hagar's official documents might have read "slave." Her role was to do what she was asked to do. She followed orders, and this time all it got her was Sarah's wrath—and Abraham's child, the reason for Sarah's wrath. True, Hagar made a crucial mistake in going overboard with the "I've got something you want" attitude. Did she think she would now be seen and known as something other than *slave* since she was carrying Abraham's baby? Sarah's harsh treatment was the shove that sent Hagar on a solo journey into the wilderness.

The angel of the Lord found a despondent Hagar by a spring. He did something that had never been done by a heavenly being—he called her by name. He did not call her slave, or woman, or any of the derogatory names Sarah may have called her. He called her name—Hagar.

Even though she had been defiant and arrogant, God sent his angel to communicate a personal message, a personal promise— to her. His message was deliberate and purposeful and doesn't even mention Abraham. God promised Hagar that—just like Abraham—she too would have many descendants.

Hagar responded by naming God "El roi"—"The God who sees me."

The same God that saw Hagar sees you. The same God that offered hope to her dejected soul offers hope to you. If you listen close you will hear God call your name to invite you on a journey of faith, fulfillment, and an eternal future with him.

Respond

What comfort can you glean as a military wife from the encounter between Hagar and the angel of the Lord?

Prayer for the journey

Lord, you see me, call me by name, and lead me out. As you go before me, help me to follow you and know your voice. Amen.

Waypoint 22

Walk before me

> When Abram was ninety-nine years old the LORD appeared to Abram and said to him, "I am God Almighty; walk before me, and be blameless, that I may make my covenant between me and you, and may multiply you greatly." Then Abram fell on his face. And God said to him, "Behold, my covenant is with you, and you shall be the father of a multitude of nations." (Genesis 17:1-4)

Reflect

"About face! Forward, march!"

Watch a group of service members in formation. Do you see a ragtag group of men and women trudging along a path? No. You see a disciplined team marching together, careful that every step is in sync. As the group marches, they are careful to listen to the superior call out commands from the front of the formation.

God Almighty visited ninety-nine year old Abraham and issued this command: "Walk before me, and be blameless." Did God mean "toe the line and do not make a mistake"? From now on would God walk behind Abraham to make sure he did not fall out of formation? Did he expect Abraham to be perfect? Was he going to hover and make sure there were no missteps? Please hear me when I say that God is not an overbearing commander waiting to yell in your ear when you blunder.

God's deepest desire for Abraham was that he would live his life so that every step he took was in sync with God's will.[21] His desire was for the natural direction of Abraham's inner compass to point toward God's presence, promises, and demands.[22]

God ordered Abraham to live a blameless life. Are you kidding? Who does that? "Blameless" sounds lofty and unattainable. But perfection is not what God asked or required of Abraham. When God commanded Abraham to live a blameless life he asked him to enjoy a wholeness of relationship with him. In other words, if Abraham fully surrendered his life to following God he would be whole and complete.[23] Abraham's life was not to be lived in fragmented pieces—one part God, one part culture, one part what he wanted to do when he wanted to do it. His life was to be wholly committed to God and God's purposes—and promises.

Respond

Do you feel out of step with God and his purposes today? Do you tend to look at life as compartmentalized into secular and spiritual? God wants your relationship with him to be whole and complete. His word to you today is, "I am God Almighty; walk before me, and be blameless."

Prayer for the journey

Almighty God, help me walk close to your side today. Keep me in step with where your Spirit leads. Amen.

Waypoint 23

A new name

> "No longer shall your name be called Abram, but your name shall be Abraham, for I have made you the father of a multitude of nations. I will make you exceedingly fruitful, and I will make you into nations, and kings shall come from you. And I will establish my covenant between me and you and your offspring after you throughout their generations for an everlasting covenant, to be God to you and to your offspring after you. And I will give to you and to your offspring after you the land of your sojournings, all the land of Canaan, for an everlasting possession, and I will be their God." (Genesis 17:5–8)

Reflect

When my husband was assigned to the School Brigade at Fort Benning, Georgia, he regularly attended the graduation for the Drill Sergeant School. The ceremonies always brought a smile to his face as he watched young soldiers accept greater leadership responsibility. He described the scene as transformational. During a typical graduation a soldier would timidly step on to the stage. There was nothing special about the soldier's carriage or countenance. The everyday camouflage cover was removed from the head and a drill sergeant hat donned in its place. That's when it happened: *transformation.* The soldier would stand taller, chest thrust out further, leaving the stage with purpose and determination. The new title, "Drill Sergeant," signaled a new era in the life of this soldier.

Thus far on our journey with Abraham, we have seen God call Abraham to respond to a promise and affirm that the promise would come. Now God guarantees the promise in covenant with Abraham. In this act (and an earlier encounter in Genesis 15:7–21), God made a formal and legally binding pledge, or grant, that he would guarantee his promise to Abraham and his offspring.

God made this promise to Abraham when he first left Ur, but in this scene it is as if Abraham finally grasped the concept. He fell on his face before God as a sign of acceptance of God's command.[24] A new era was signaled when God said, "No longer shall your name be called Abram, but your name shall be Abraham, for I have made you the father of a multitude of nations" (Genesis 17:5).

In biblical times names were much more than identification labels. They signified a person's character or destiny. This change in name for Abraham (and soon for Sarah), symbolized the internal change that had taken place.[25] The names were changed by God himself and represented God's seal on their future in his divine plan. As they walked closer to God, their priorities changed, and so did their role in history.[26]

Respond

An encounter with God Almighty changes a person. How have you changed since becoming a Christ-follower? What steps are you taking to keep your relationship with God growing strong?

Prayer for the journey

Increase my knowledge of you, Lord. Help me know your will and walk in a manner worthy of you. Amen.

Waypoint 24

A unique birth announcement

Read Genesis 18:9–15

> The LORD said to Abraham, "Why did Sarah laugh and say, 'Shall I indeed bear a child, now that I am old?' Is anything too hard for the Lord? At the appointed time I will return to you, about this time next year, and Sarah shall have a son." (Genesis 18:13–14)

Reflect

Perhaps you have seen clever birth announcements from military families. Such creative notices of a new addition bring a smile to my face. For instance:

"Reporting for Duty (projected date of birth)."

"I'm being promoted to big sister/brother." (Sign held by older child.)

"The Jenkins family will have a new recruit (projected date of birth)."

The announcement from the three strangers who visited Abraham's camp that a child would be born to Abraham and Sarah did not just bring a smile—it brought a guffaw of laughter. Honestly, can you blame Sarah for laughing? That sure would be my response if I was a ninety-plus year old woman.[27]

Sarah's laughter was met with one of the greatest statements in Scripture: "Is anything too hard for the Lord?" Such words challenge the core of faith. The words held no rebuke, but were rather a gentle reminder that God knew Sarah's name, as well as her thoughts, and he—and only he—was able to bring such an impossible event to pass.[28]

Through this unusual visit Sarah was drawn into full ownership of her part in the covenant promise.[29] For Sarah to become pregnant was not reasonable, but faith transcends reason. Although her body was no longer naturally capable of becoming pregnant, God extended a personal invitation for her to become the mother of nations. A door of hope for the future was opened to Sarah that day, and it should bring a smile to each of our faces.[30] That door of hope remains open for each of us through Christ, the ultimate fulfillment of the promise to Abraham.

Respond

Has God ever led you to do something you thought was impossible? Are you facing something that seems impossible today? "Is anything too hard for God?" is not meant to be a verse we claim in order to change our circumstances. God can certainly change circumstances, but sometimes the toughest thing for us is to accept our circumstances and grow through them.[31]

Prayer for the journey

Thank you for being the God of the impossible. I bring my list of impossibilities to you and ask for your grace to look at them through the lens of trust. Increase my faith in you as the one who is able to do so much more than I can ever ask for, or even think of. Amen. (Ephesians 3:20)

Waypoint 25

Because of Abraham

Read Genesis 18:16–19:29

So it was that, when God destroyed the cities of the valley, God remembered Abraham … (Genesis 19:29a)

Reflect

"If it were not for _____, I would never have made it as a military wife."

Does a name, or names, immediately come to mind when you look at this blank? Without hesitation, I would write the name Sandra. Sandra taught me about the fundamentals of military life. I learned from her gracious example, as well as her responses to my myriad questions. The most important thing she taught me, however, was how to care for people in my sphere of influence. Sandra was the wife of the battalion commander at my husband's first military assignment. She introduced herself the day we moved into military quarters. Soon afterward, she invited me to meet with her each week to pray for the military families in the battalion. In retrospect, I'm not sure what I expected from a commander's wife, but I can say with conviction that prayer meetings were not on the list.

Sandra's call to prayer illustrates a Christian principle: Christian maturity exhibits itself in caring for people. Abraham's request of God to spare the city of Sodom was a good indicator that his relationship with God was growing. The situation in Sodom was beyond serious. The strangers who had just announced the wonderful news about the birth of a baby now announced horrific news about the destruction of a city. Abraham did not want to accept God's plan for such severe judgment. There were people in the city. He had relatives in that city—remember Lot?

Here we see a baffled Abraham standing before a patient God who was waiting for Abraham to intercede on behalf of people in crisis.[32] Abraham found his voice. This time he did not use it to lie about the identity of his wife, or laugh because he could not believe he would be a father. He used his voice to petition God on behalf of the needs of others. At first, he seemed a little hesitant to make such a request of God, but his tentative appeal became bolder as he asked for mercy even if only ten righteous people were to be found in the city.

Sadly, there were not even ten, but because of Abraham, Lot and his family were escorted out of town before the destruction came. Your prayers on behalf of others make a difference. Who will eventually write your name in their blank?

Respond

Do you regularly pray for the service members and families in your husband's military unit? Is there someone who would join you in praying together consistently?

Prayer for the journey

Lord, help me show my love for others through consistent prayer on their behalf. Thank you for the privilege of prayer and the promise that you are a God who hears. Amen.

Waypoint 26

Three steps forward, two steps back

Read Genesis 20 and Genesis 21:22–34

> And Abraham said of Sarah his wife, "She is my sister."
> (Genesis 20:2a)

Reflect

"I know better! How could I make the same mistake again?"

Can you relate? Have you asked yourself how you could do something you thought you would never repeat? Welcome to the human condition. I call it the three steps forward, two steps back syndrome. Abraham knew something about this pattern.

After the destruction of Sodom, Abraham traveled south. Again he gave in to his fear that trouble would come from a foreign king. He went into panic mode yet again and lied about Sarah, yet again. Didn't we just read about him becoming more mature in his faith—praying for others—believing God for a son in his old age? Why would he put the promise God made to him in jeopardy by allowing his wife to be taken into a king's harem, yet again?

Yes, we can see a pattern with Abraham, but we can also see a pattern with God: When we take steps backward, God is always willing to take steps forward. In this case, God appeared to King Abimelech in a dream and told him that Sarah was a married woman and, in essence, that Abraham was an object of God's special care.

The dream did not keep the king from asking Abraham a pointed question: "What have you done to us?"

Abraham made excuses: "I thought you would kill me." "Technically, she is my half-sister." "This all happened because God made me leave my home."

Excuses, excuses. I know them too well when I fail to trust God. What about you?

The fact that Abraham failed to trust God is really no surprise. The surprise is the merciful way God intervened. Abraham acknowledged God's intervention and mercy by planting a tree as a landmark of God's grace. What a perfect symbol of the journey thus far. The longer he journeyed with God the more his faith was rooted in God's trustworthy character.[33]

Respond

What are some symbols you have that attest to your relationship with God as rooted and growing? Are there steps you take or can take to protect you from repeating sinful patterns?

Prayer for the journey

Lord, thank you for being a God who is faithful even when I am faithless. Your mercy and grace are amazing. Help me stand firm and trust in your power and not my own. Amen.

Waypoint 27
The Lord takes note of you

Read Genesis 21:1–7

Then the LORD took note of Sarah as he had said, and the LORD did for Sarah as he had promised. (Genesis 21:1 NASB)

Reflect

Do you understand the significance of the opening of Genesis 21? Take a look: "Then the Lord took note of Sarah ..."

When it came time for the promised son to be born, the focus of God was not on Abraham, but on Sarah. The words of this verse refer to the direct intervention of God.[34] Beyond the realm of human possibility Sarah became a mother. God focused his attention on Sarah and her part in the fulfillment of the promise that she would birth a son.[35] God made an appointment with Sarah a year earlier—and sisters, God keeps his appointments!

God took note of a young military wife named Julie. She and her chaplain husband met in Bible college. Julie graduated a few years before he did and then worked full-time to support his seminary education. She patiently waited until *finally* they headed into what she thought would be joint ministry.

Her husband became a chaplain, and Julie was disillusioned as he sailed into his role and there was no place for her. He wore the uniform and was fulfilled in his work, and that made Julie angry.

"I remember shaking my fist at God," she told me, "and asking him why it took a college degree to wash someone's underwear! (I know, I know ... not my best moment.) But I found the end of my rope and relinquished desire for my own ministry. A heart that has come to its end is a heart God can use, and he has used me! By the time we left our first assignment, I was convinced God had assigned *me* to that place and my husband was the tag-along. In every posting, God has given *me* assignments. I have permission to minister to the people that I do *because* my husband is in the military; it would never work otherwise. God has given me favor and influence and a more powerful ministry than I ever envisioned. All glory to God!"

You can find hope in the story of God's attention and intervention in the life of Sarah and in the life of a military sister like Julie. Your purposes in God's plan as a wife are as important as God's purposes for your military husband. God can assign your husband to the place you are supposed to be for his purpose. Be encouraged today—the Lord takes note of you!

Respond

Do you ever feel marginalized as a military wife? How can you encourage other military wives to know that God takes note of them?

Prayer for the journey

Lord, thank you for taking note of me! Help me to take note of others and affirm their value to you. Amen.

Waypoint 28
Test of faith

After these things God tested Abraham and said to him, "Abraham!" And he said, "Here I am." He said, "Take your son, your only son Isaac, whom you love, and go to the land of Moriah, and offer him there as a burnt offering on one of the mountains of which I shall tell you." (Genesis 22:1–2)

Reflect

Fortunately, there is no test to become a military wife. Can you imagine the questions: Fill-in-the-blank rank structure? Match letter groups to the correct acronyms? Multiple choice answers for military protocol or history? An essay question on "why I want to be the best military wife ever"? Yes, I'm glad there were no tests because I doubt I would have passed.

The reader of Genesis 22 is let in on a secret: there is going to be a test. Abraham was not aware of the upcoming examination—much more than a spiritual pop quiz. Finally, the promised child Isaac had been born. The Scripture jumps from his miraculous birth to the potential nation he represented, now in jeopardy. How could God ask for such a sacrifice?

We watch the father-son trek up to Mount Moriah. God's instruction to Abraham was to *go*. It was the same word used when God first called Abraham to leave all he held dear in his homeland and go to a place God would show him. Now the word required him to *go* and offer the Lord what he loved most. This time it was not home or land. This time it was his son—his only son. God had met him at each turn in the road. Would this time be any different?

The journey to Moriah meant Abraham had to lay his expectations and hopes on the altar along with his son. He had to ask if his faith was focused on the hope wrapped up in his only son, or if his faith was focused on God.[36] Was Abraham willing to follow God if there was nothing in it for him? I must ask the same question when tests come to me. Tests of my faith force me to rely on God. Abraham's experience with God thus far allowed him to go to a most difficult place with the trust that God would provide exactly what was needed at the exact time.

Respond

None of us gets an exemption from the tests of life. The question Abraham had to answer is the same one each of us must answer: Will you serve God regardless of your circumstances?

Prayer for the journey

Lord, help my relationship with you to grow stronger in the midst of challenging circumstances that test my faith. Amen.

Waypoint 29

Memorial to a dedicated wife and mother

Read Genesis 23

> Sarah lived 127 years; these were the years of the life of Sarah. (Genesis 23:1)

Reflect

On a beautiful hilltop overlooking the Blue Ridge Mountains is a tombstone inscribed with the name of my mother-in-law. Her final resting place is in the Georgia National Cemetery, where one day her veteran husband will join her. Our nation has set aside beautiful pieces of land to honor and remember those who serve our country through military service. The military wife and her service alongside her husband are included in this gracious memorial.

Sarah came to the end of her life and there was no place to bury her. Was Abraham to take her body back to Ur? Should he accept the offer of a gift from the inhabitants of the land? What was a sojourner to do?

Abraham strategically negotiated the purchase of ground on which to bury Sarah. Isn't it remarkable that the first piece of property Abraham owned in the Promised Land was a plot to bury his wife? He realized the importance of a place for successive generations to memorialize their faith. God led them to this land that would one day be theirs.[37] Sarah's grave was in essence a spiritual beachhead for the borders the Lord would expand to become the nation of Israel.

Sarah was buried east of Mamre, a place where some of her happiest memories had taken place. It was here that the Lord promised her she would give birth to a child. It was here the sojourner rested, no longer a stranger.[38]

Sarah did not know the impact she would have on others. We read of the significance of her death, but it was her life that held the greatest impact. Did you know Sarah is the only woman in Scripture whose lifespan is mentioned? That says to me that God takes note when we live a life devoted to him, and others. The words we say and the deeds we do establish a beachhead of God's plan and will.

Perhaps one day I will join my mother-in-law on that memorial hill in North Georgia. Until then, it's the people I bless while I'm alive that will make my life a memorial. You do not know the blessing you are to others. Go out and be a blessing today! God will not forget you!

Respond

Our nation does not forget a military wife. Abraham did not forget Sarah. God will not forget you. With this assurance, what courageous actions will you take today?

Prayer for the journey

Lord, thank you for a nation that does not forget the service of a military wife. Most of all, I thank you for being a God who does not forget me. Help me today to be the blessing you've called me to be to those I meet. Amen.

Waypoint 30
Satisfied with life

Read

> These are all the years of Abraham's life that he lived, one hundred and seventy-five years. Abraham breathed his last and died in a ripe old age, an old man and satisfied with life; and he was gathered to his people. (Genesis 25:7–8 NASB)

Reflect

What could be a better obituary than to read a person died at a good old age and lived a full and satisfied life?

What does it mean to be satisfied with life? To enjoy the journey? To have no regrets? To let go of the things that would cause remorse?

Abraham's life was not easy. He spent most of his life without a place to call home. He knew the pain of loss. He knew the impatience of waiting. He knew the disappointment of personal failure. He knew the frustration of fear. He knew the anguish of sacrifice. Yet he ended his life satisfied and content. He was far from perfect, but he left a legacy of faith because he learned to live by faith. He learned something you and I can learn as we journey through life.

In studying the life of Abraham and his journey with God, it is easy to be impressed with his obedience and his sense of adventure, but I am most impressed with the role God played in the journey. God was the one who always initiated, helped, and waited.[39] He revealed himself step by step as Abraham traveled. Through the relationship Abraham was invited to have with God, all nations of the world would be blessed as they were shown what God was like.[40] Abraham's satisfaction was not in the life he lived, but in the God he served.

A military survey recently reported that Army spouses are increasingly satisfied with their way of life, supportive of their soldiers' careers, and generally coping better with deployments. In fact, they want to stay in the Army more than their soldier spouses.[41] There is never a way to know if a survey like this represents the opinion of an entire group. I do know, however, that when it comes time to depart this life, our satisfaction will not be based on a husband's rank, a retirement home, or money in the bank. Satisfaction, at that point, will come when, like Abraham, we know our relationship with the Lord is established and sure.

Respond

How satisfied are you with military life? How does your relationship with God affect your overall satisfaction with life?

Prayer for the journey

You make known to me the path of life; in your presence there is fullness of joy; at your right hand are pleasures forevermore. (Psalm 16:11) Amen.

Journey 2

Dedicated to God's Mission

Introduction

At nineteen years of age, Janna married Billy, her high school sweetheart. Soon after the wedding, Billy's employer laid him off and he could not find another job. In desperation, Billy found a military recruiting office and signed up to join the Army. Billy's first assignment, following basic training, was an infantry unit that deployed almost immediately after his arrival.

Janna now lives in a state far from home and is being introduced to a strange culture called the military. She is on her own to navigate a new way of life. She does not have a church background, so she will not likely seek out a church to fill the void in her life.

Who will be the hands, feet, and voice for Jesus to the Jannas in the U.S. military population? If you are a Christ follower, *you* are the hands, feet, and voice of Jesus wherever you find yourself.

This thirty-day journey, "Dedicated to God's Mission," explores what it means to be a dedicated Christ follower on mission for God wherever he takes us. Together, we will join Jesus and his disciples on a trek through the Gospel of Mark where we will see a succinct picture of Jesus as a man on a mission. There is a sense of urgency and purpose in what Jesus did and where Jesus went. We can learn much from his attitude of love and service, and we gain immeasurably when we accept the gift of eternal life he offers through his death and resurrection.

At each day's Waypoint, don't forget to begin by asking God: "Open my eyes, that I may behold wondrous things out of your law" (Psalm 119:18).

Why don't you think about joining with some fellow sojourners to study God's Word together?

Welcome to the journey!

Waypoint 1

Good news worth retweeting

> The beginning of the gospel of Jesus Christ, the Son of God. (Mark 1:1)

Good news travels fast.

Social psychologists at the University of Pennsylvania analyzed social media habits and found people more likely to share good news than bad.[1] Twitter has become a place where news breaks. Since it launched, the highest compliment for users of this social media platform is to have one of your 140-character messages "retweeted"—shared by other users.

You may be surprised to learn that Pope Francis has the most frequently retweeted Twitter account in the world (@pontifex). This may be an indicator that people are hungry for good news and truth. The good news retweeted from the Pope's account may also indicate the interest people have in God.

These thoughts about Twitter were prompted by the first verse in the Gospel according to Mark, which reads like a modern-day tweet:

> @GospelMark: "The beginning of the gospel of Jesus Christ, the Son of God." #hehasgoodnews #heisgoodnews

In his first sentence Mark alerts his readers to what is to come in his account of Jesus. He provides a short summary of the acts of Christ and the identity of Christ. It is as if he cannot wait to begin to share the good news he has come to know and love. The word *gospel* is from an Old English word meaning *good news,* the translation of the Greek term for these accounts of Jesus. The Greeks used the word for gospel to declare a military victory, announce a royal birth, or broadcast a political triumph.[2] Mark uses the word with the intention of passing on the good news about Jesus. More importantly, he intends to proclaim that Jesus *is* the good news.

Today we begin a thirty-day journey with Jesus and his disciples to see what it means to be on mission for God—which means, in effect, to retweet Jesus. No, I do not mean sending 140-character comments about Jesus into cyberspace, although that could be an effective method of sharing Christ. I am talking about the good news of Jesus making such a difference in your life that he can be seen in your thoughts, words, and actions. Sisters, Jesus is good news worth retweeting!

Respond

What does it mean to you to be on *mission* for God? When you consider your life as a follower of Christ, how are you sharing the good news of Jesus?

Prayer for the journey

Lord, today let me be a conduit of you and your good news. Amen.

Waypoint 2

Prepared for the journey

> As it is written in Isaiah the prophet, "Behold, I send my messenger before your face, who will prepare your way, the voice of one crying in the wilderness: 'Prepare the way of the Lord, make his paths straight.'" (Mark 1:1–3)

Nellie sat in a group of military wives at a retreat center in the Rocky Mountains. "I *never* wanted to be a military wife!" she said:

> I knew nothing about the military, but I did know it was not for me. The constant change, the many moves, and short roots did not feel comfortable. I grew up in the same house until my freshman year of high school when my mom remarried. Our family moved into a new house about a mile away to provide the new marriage a fresh space. I remember sobbing as I sat on the floor surrounded by stacks of boxes in my childhood room. Moving from that home was very difficult. That move, however, began a series of moves that ultimately allowed me to embrace the nomadic routine of being part of a military family. God used those difficult moves to prepare me for what was ahead. I am so grateful for his path of preparation!

Today, Nellie thrives as a wife, mom, entrepreneur, and follower of Christ. Through her web-based business, she connects other military wives with services in new military communities and makes their adjustment easier. She helps "prepare the way" for other military wives and God is using her as a voice of encouragement.

God is all about preparation. Before he sent Jesus into the world, God used John the Baptist to prepare the way. Even before that, he spoke through prophets like Isaiah and Zechariah with the news that Messiah would come. He prepared Jesus for his public ministry through the life he lived in a small village with an ordinary family among ordinary people. Similarly, God prepares us for the mission he has for us. He uses our past experiences to make us into people ready to serve him where we are. As a Christ follower, you are not in a military community to waste or bide time; you are there for a mission. You can't always see how your mission will play out, but you can rest assured that the Lord can and will use you if you have a willing heart. Just ask Nellie!

Respond
Preparation for any mission is a process. In what ways can you look back and see how the Lord prepared you for military life?

Prayer for the journey
Lord, you are a God of preparation. Help me see the ways you have prepared me to be on mission for you in this place, for this season. Amen.

Waypoint 3

At your service

> John appeared, baptizing in the wilderness and pro-
> claiming a baptism of repentance for the forgiveness
> of sins...And he preached, saying, "After me comes he
> who is mightier than I, the strap of whose sandals I am
> not worthy to stoop down and untie. I have baptized
> you with water, but he will baptize you with the Holy
> Spirit." In those days Jesus came from Nazareth of Gali-
> lee and was baptized by John in the Jordan (Mark 1:4-9).

Reflect

"Who, me? Are you sure you're asking the right person?" I feel
embarrassed when I think of my response to an invitation to
serve punch at a welcome coffee for the incoming commanding
general's wife. I know it sounds old school to write about serving
punch at a formal gathering, but trust me—this was a big deal.
Formal protocol was more the norm than it is today, and it was
an honor to participate. I was brand new to this military wife gig
and to describe myself as insecure is an understatement. What if
I went to this formal function and spilled something, or forgot
a military acronym, or made a complete fool of myself in any
myriad of ways? I felt inadequate to serve.

To compare my fear of accidently baptizing a general's wife
with punch to John baptizing Jesus is certainly out of balance,
but the emotion attached to feeling inadequate is universal.
Jesus approached John to baptize him and John clearly felt
inadequate to serve in that capacity. Yet, to baptize Jesus was
part of the mission John was to fulfill. His was the task to

introduce the Messiah to the world. He was inadequate, but in his service he was obedient. John dedicated himself to do God's will by doing as Jesus asked, even as Jesus dedicated himself to do God's will in leaving heaven to come to earth. The picture is one of obedient service: John served Jesus as Jesus committed himself to be a servant of all. Jesus invites us to participate in his mission of service.

We should feel inadequate to serve the way John and Jesus did, yet the call to be obedient requires that we allow Jesus to serve through us, and he is beyond adequate. Remember, the first trait God is looking for in someone to be used in service is not competence, but obedience. The self-declared obedient servant of God, the apostle Paul, revealed the secret of his competence when he said, *"I can do all things through him who strengthens me"* (Philippians 4:13).

Respond

How are you involved in serving others? What can you do to combat feelings of inadequacy that may keep you from serving?

Prayer for the journey

I desire to do your will, O God. Open my eyes to see opportunities to serve others today. Amen.

Waypoint 4

You can do it!

And when he came up out of the water, immediately he saw the heavens being torn open and the Spirit descending on him like a dove. And a voice came from heaven, "You are my beloved Son; with you I am well pleased." (Mark 1:10–11)

Reflect

"We can do it!" are the words emblazoned on the iconic World War II motivational poster featuring a woman who became known as Rosie the Riveter. As America's men went to fight in the war, women were recruited to fill the colossal gaps in the factory workforce. Rosie the Riveter was an empowering figure as she challenged women to carry out an important mission for the nation.[4]

The dramatic pronouncement from heaven here in Mark 1 is a moment of heavenly empowerment. Jesus is commissioned by God to do the work for which he was prepared. The Spirit confirms that he is equipped for the role.[5] In essence, Jesus is reminded with words from his Father that he is not alone. "You are my beloved Son; with you I am well pleased" are words of approval and empowerment. The words communicate the competence of Jesus to fulfill the mission before him.[6] In a loose paraphrase, God is saying: "You can do it!" Jesus could do it because he is the Son of God. He could do it because the Holy Spirit empowered and equipped him.

Empowerment is that intangible something that enables me to hold my head up high, walk with confidence, and do something positive with the influence that is mine. When I'm empowered, I have that Rosie the Riveter attitude of "I can do it!" As a Christ follower I know that my "can do" must come from reliance on the Holy Spirit's work within me. Thank God that the same power that equipped and empowered Jesus for ministry is available to each of us!

Sisters, God does not send us on mission on our own. He empowers us. He equips us. He says to us, "With my help, you can do it!"

Respond

Think of a time you felt empowered. Write some of the words that come to mind in your journal. What do these Scriptures have to say about empowerment?

- Deuteronomy 31:6
- Acts 1:8
- 2 Corinthians 12:9
- 1 John 4:4

Prayer for the journey

Father, help me walk in your "can do" Spirit today. Thank you for the reminder that you are with me. Use me in your service. Amen.

Waypoint 5

It's tempting

> The Spirit immediately drove him out into the wilderness. And he was in the wilderness forty days, being tempted by Satan. And he was with the wild animals, and the angels were ministering to him. (Mark 1:12–13)

Reflect

I don't like to talk about temptation. I'm, well, tempted to ignore it and not think about the reality of its effect on my soul. I could even boast about the mega-temptations that do not make it past my line of sight and make me feel pretty good about myself. If I did, I would be succumbing to the temptation of deception. Temptation is a reality of life for everyone. Even Jesus was tempted.

The road toward mission fulfillment for Jesus took him to the wilderness. For the Hebrews, the wilderness was branded as God's proving ground.[7] It was dry, dusty, difficult, and dangerous—as in "he was with the wild animals" dangerous. He was sent there by God, full of the Holy Spirit, to be tested. In this desolate place Satan set out to thwart the mission of Jesus and compel him to be disobedient to the will of the Father.[8]

This was no *Survivor: Judean Wilderness Edition* to see if Jesus could "outwit, outplay, outlast" Satan. Jesus was not tested to merely see if he could survive. It can be hard for us to comprehend that Jesus as God faced a genuine test. Scripture is clear that Jesus is both God and man; we can understand his humanness being tested because our humanness is tested every day. Temptation and testing come to us not because we are sinners, but because we are human. In this barren place Jesus came face to face with his humanity.

Satan's goal was to get Jesus to deny his dependence on the Father and to act on his own.[9] Is there room for a little true confession? I'm tempted to do that every single day! I am tempted to provide for myself, protect myself, and promote myself—and so was Jesus! He understands my temptations and I know his victory over temptation offers hope for me. I overcome temptation not only by following the example of Christ, but also by inviting the victorious Christ to live in me.

Respond
How can the areas of provision, protection, and promotion be areas of temptation? In what ways are you tempted to provide for, protect, and promote yourself?

Prayer for the journey
Lord, it is comforting to know you understand temptation and times of testing. I pray for wisdom to recognize temptations and for faith to trust your power to overcome them. In your mighty name, Amen.

Waypoint 6
The first assignment

Read

> Now after John was arrested, Jesus came into Galilee, proclaiming the gospel of God, and saying, "The time is fulfilled, and the kingdom of God is at hand; repent and believe in the gospel." (Mark 1:14–15)

Reflect

I felt let down when my husband's first military orders arrived for Ft. Benning, Georgia, otherwise known as "Ft. Beginning" because of the basic training that takes place there. I was one of those who bought into the line "join the military and see the world." Here we were being sent to my husband's home state of Georgia. When we arrived in Columbus it seemed so ordinary—and hot. Oh my, was Columbus, Georgia a hot and humid place to live.

The message of Mark 1:14–15 prepares the reader for what could be a thrilling event. The stage is set with a voice from heaven, a battle with Satan, and a proclamation that "the kingdom of God is at hand!" Instead of a thrilling event of pomp and pageantry following all this drama, there is a walk into the backwater region of Galilee.[10] You would think Jesus would start his ministry in Jerusalem, the epicenter of religious activity. He eventually journeyed there, but that was not where he started his ministry. Jesus started in Galilee, a place symbolic of day-to-day life.[11] He went to where the common people were, in what could be described as his own home state.[12]

My fellow seekers of exotic, big, out-of-the-ordinary days, don't miss the lesson here: God uses us in the ordinary places and in everyday life. Because of God's presence in those days and those places, "ordinary ceases to exist."[13] It is easy to belittle the ordinary, but life is full of ordinary days and places. If we don't see the possibilities, we will miss the mission.

Jesus says ordinary things like sharing food, drink, clothes, or a visit become extraordinary acts of service when done on his behalf (Matthew 25:35–36). We are invited to be God's hands, feet, and voice in those ordinary places. It was good enough for Jesus; it is good enough for me. What about you?

Respond

How do we minimize ordinary days or places? How does underestimating the ordinary keep us from mission and service?

Prayer for the journey

Lord, forgive me when I do not see the gift of an ordinary day. Help me to be your hands, feet, and voice. Amen.

Waypoint 7

Follow me

> Passing alongside the Sea of Galilee, he saw Simon and Andrew the brother of Simon casting a net into the sea, for they were fishermen. And Jesus said to them, "Follow me, and I will make you become fishers of men." And immediately they left their nets and followed him. And going on a little farther, he saw James the son of Zebedee and John his brother, who were in their boat mending the nets. And immediately he called them, and they left their father Zebedee in the boat with the hired servants and followed him. (Mark 1:16–20)

Reflect

These few short verses stop me in my tracks. Think about it. Jesus came up to these fishermen, told them to leave everything to follow him—and they did. They walked away from their family and economic security. They laid everything down. They left. They followed. Even though the Gospel of John lets us know these men encountered Jesus earlier through the ministry of John the Baptist, their spontaneous, immediate, and unconditional response to Jesus' invitation, "Follow me," makes a powerful statement about the authority of Jesus.[14]

Spend any time on a military installation and you will hear commands issued and followed. In the military it is the authority of rank that turns a request into a command.

The words of Jesus to Simon, Andrew, James, and John were heard much like a sharp military command.[15] Authority is what these men heard when Christ issued a call to follow him.

Somehow these fishermen received the words of Jesus with a confidence that they would be able to become what Jesus offered. That's faith. Sisters, if Jesus calls you, he will enable you.

These socially insignificant folks would fail and disappoint him, but their role was crucial to the success of his mission. Through them, the kingdom of God was made known throughout the world. I often feel insignificant and I certainly fail and disappoint him, but my role is no less crucial to this kingdom mission. He wants to use us to make his name known. Let's follow!

Respond

These disciples were flawed but willing followers who can show us what it looks like to be a disciple of Christ. In them, we see three fundamental elements of discipleship: (1) a relationship with Jesus; (2) active promotion of his mission; and (3) total commitment to his cause.[16]

Where are you on this discipleship journey? Do you have a relationship with him? Are you actively promoting his mission? Are you committed totally to his cause?

Prayer for the journey

Lord, help me to daily grow in my relationship with you. Show me how to promote your mission in my sphere of influence and make me totally committed to your cause to reconcile others to you.

Waypoint 8

Why I serve

Now Simon's mother-in-law lay ill with a fever, and immediately they told him about her. And he came and took her by the hand and lifted her up, and the fever left her, and she began to serve them. (Mark 1:30–31)

"I serve because I want to give back a small portion of what I have been given. I want my children to know what it means to live in the 'land of the free' and the 'home of the brave.' I want others to realize the tremendous honor they have to live in a country based on the highest ideals man has ever seen."[17]

With these words, Air Force officer Daniel Gernert shares the reason for his service in the military. In general, "service" is the action of helping others. It is good practice to review our motivation to serve. Whether we are serving under oath, volunteering in a group, or simply helping others, our motivation is an important factor in making our service meaningful.

Peter's mother-in-law could have taught a class on "Why I serve." Her story starts with a fever. In the ancient world a fever was not considered a mild condition—as in, "Take two aspirin and call me in the morning." In those days a fever was seen as an inner fire caused by a curse or a demon that could only be extinguished by God.[18] Enter Jesus to the house where Peter's mother-in-law is laid low with a fever.

From what I've read about Peter, even if he lived today with the ability to text ahead to his wife and give a heads-up that he was bringing someone home, I doubt he would have taken advantage of the technology. He was quite impulsive. Case in point: He just left his job to follow a wandering preacher! Imagine the miracle missed if he had been able to call ahead and warn his wife and was told, "The house is a mess and mom is sick. No how, no way, do you bring someone here!"

Thank goodness that was not the case. Jesus came, takes mom by the hand, lifts her up, and the fever leaves her. What does she do in response? "She began to serve them." Her service is not something menial or demeaning but rather a sign of her physical and mental wholeness. The actions of this woman are proof positive that her healing was complete and her heart was open to Jesus.[19] This is a model for any follower of Christ: when he transforms a person, the outpouring of that transformation is service.

Respond

Why do you serve others? Is it for social interaction? Is it to be recognized? Is it to do the "right" thing? If your reason for service is not founded in relationship with the Lord then you are missing an area of fulfillment that God intends for you.

Prayer for the journey

Lord, I desire to serve you with faithfulness. Help me to show your love through my service to others. Amen.

Waypoint 9

Zero dark thirty

> And rising very early in the morning, while it was still dark, he departed and went out to a desolate place, and there he prayed. (Mark 1:35)

"Some mornings I feel like if getting up early was an object, I would break it, burn it, and bury it where it could never be found again." I read these words on a greeting card and shook my head in agreement.

Anyone associated with the military knows about getting up at zero dark thirty. A study published in the *Journal of Applied Social Psychology* reported that early risers are more proactive, get better grades in school, anticipate problems and try to minimize them, have more time to exercise, eat healthier, and enjoy more time doing what they love to do.[20] As a self-professed night owl I sarcastically say, "good for them."

In Mark 1:35 we're told Jesus quietly rose before anyone else. His itinerary had been intense and he knew more was to come. He went outside and found a remote spot. The point was not the hour of the day, but the act of the hour. Even though he must have been tired after a demanding day of ministry, his sense of mission compelled him to find a place free of distraction for prayer.[21]

No distractions—are you kidding me? It sounds like a small thing, but depending on the season of life it can be impossible. I realize from this scene, however, that if Jesus needed to make time for prayer, so must I. If he prayed in order to live a life empowered by God, so must I.[22] I don't know about you, but I can't do this thing called life without the help of the Lord. I get overwhelmed too easily. I get focused on me too much. I forget too often that I have a divine purpose.

There are no medals for rising early. As we establish a habit of prayer, the thing we have to remember is prayer is not about performance. It is about taking time to talk to God, and making time to listen to him. God's schedule is not so full that he cannot communicate with you whenever you come to him. It's not the time, place, or length, but that we do it.

Respond

The same God who gave Jesus strength, encouragement, and guidance for his earthly mission is available to us through prayer. Do you have a set time or place for being alone with God? What are some ways you incorporate prayer into your day?

Prayer for the journey

Lord, help me live in your presence every moment of this day. Thank you for the privilege to communicate with you. Guide me on the journey called today.

Waypoint 10

Four friends and a roof

> And when he returned to Capernaum after some days, it was reported that he was at home. And many were gathered together, so that there was no more room, not even at the door. And he was preaching the word to them. And they came, bringing to him a paralytic carried by four men. And when they could not get near him because of the crowd, they removed the roof above him, and when they had made an opening, they let down the bed on which the paralytic lay. And when Jesus saw their faith, he said to the paralytic, "Son, your sins are forgiven." (Mark 2:1–5)

Reflect

Military wives are the most resourceful and creative people you can find. As one put it, "We could give MacGyver a run for his money."[23] Read Mark 2:1–5 and you could believe a Roman soldier's wife was outside the crowded house telling the paralytic man's friends how to get him to Jesus. Lowering him through the roof is the kind of creative solution a military wife would use.

As a military wife, I also identify with the friendship represented in this story. Military wives make the best friends. The paralytic man's friends were willing to go to extreme measures to get their friend to Jesus. They did not let the barrier of the crowd intimidate them. They did not let the barrier of the roof intimidate them. They dug out the mud roof, removed the wood crossbeams, and lowered their disabled friend into the presence of Jesus. What an entrance!

I cannot help but be inspired by this man's creative friends. In Mark 2:5, notice that Jesus *saw their faith*. There is no mention of words of faith being spoken, but there is an action of faith demonstrated by the friends. Their action said they believed in the healing power of Jesus and they got creative in finding a way for their friend to encounter that power.[24] The paralytic was made whole that day. Jesus healed his body, but he also forgave his sins.

Sisters, we are on a mission to point people to Christ so they can be made whole. God can use our faith to make a difference in the lives of others.

Respond

What model do the friends of the paralytic man provide? Do you have friends like that in your life? How are you a friend like that to others?

Prayer for the journey

Lord, thank you for the gift of friendship. Help me to be willing to break through barriers to share you with my friends. Amen.

Waypoint 11

Don't shoot the messenger

> And as he passed by, he saw Levi the son of Alphaeus sitting at the tax booth, and he said to him, "Follow me." And he rose and followed him. And as he reclined at the table in his house, many tax collectors and sinners were reclining with Jesus and his disciples, for there were many who followed him. (Mark 2:14–15)

Reflect

Recently I was incorrectly charged for a medical test. It took months of frustrating phone calls to finally resolve the issue. Through the myriad of calls, I had to continually remind myself not to "shoot the messenger" with angry words. The individual who called me did not personally make the mistake, but was just the messenger of bad news.

"Don't shoot the messenger" might have been words spoken regularly by Levi, the man described in Mark 2:14–15. As a tax collector, he did not set the tax rates, but was given the job to accept toll money as people crossed from one part of the kingdom into the other.[25] Many Jews who made the regular trip back and forth could remember when there was no toll to pay, and in their resentment let the complaints fly toward the toll collector. Then one day someone passed by Levi's booth, looked at him and said, "Follow me." Jesus did not shoot the messenger. Instead he extended a hand and changed his life.

Levi followed Jesus and even pulled together some of his other tax collector friends so they could meet him too. The actions of Jesus did not sit well with the religious leaders, but he did not apologize for his choice of companions. No, he made the point that not only was it acceptable for him to spend time with such people, it was the purpose of his mission (v. 16–17).

We all have a natural tendency to associate with those like us, especially those who have the same beliefs. While Jesus spent the majority of his time with his disciples, he also went out of his way to associate with people considered outsiders so he could address their spiritual needs.

We need to be in close community with those who will deepen our walk with Christ. We must also reach beyond these circles and befriend those who need the love of Christ. You and I may face some criticism for our choice of friends, just as Jesus did, but we are to love them with God's love, and we may have the privilege of being the messenger God uses to introduce them to the Savior.

Respond

Are you meaningfully connected with people who do not share your Christian beliefs? If not, how can you make a new connection?

Prayer for the journey

Lord, show me how to be a friend. Amen.

Waypoint 12

Vive la différence

> And the scribes of the Pharisees, when they saw that he was eating with sinners and tax collectors, said to his disciples, "Why does he eat with tax collectors and sinners?" And when Jesus heard it, he said to them, "Those who are well have no need of a physician, but those who are sick. I came not to call the righteous, but sinners." (Mark 2:16–17)

Reflect

I don't know about you, but I grew up in a pretty homogenous town. I liken it to being enveloped in bubble wrap. Mine was a protected upbringing where anyone different stood out. When my husband became a Soldier, he blended into any camouflage group. My little boys would grab onto the boots of any Soldier and look up for "daddy" because everyone looked like daddy. But even with this visual uniformity, military life was different. Different as in: different people, different attitudes, a different way of doing things. And the diversity caused unanticipated culture shock.

I soon learned to appreciate different! Every military community brings together different groups—people from different religions, even Christians from different denominations with different practices. I learned that "different" did not mean it was time to draw division lines, but to embrace differences and be enriched by encountering something new.

The Jewish leaders who criticized Jesus for eating with "tax collectors and sinners" did not like "different." The fact that Jesus shared a table with those who were considered outsiders made them suspicious of him.[26] Their job was to ensure everyone followed the same religious rules, and this made Jesus' actions unacceptable.[27] They did not understand that Jesus did not just eat with people who were different for the sake of being different. He knew that even—especially—those who were different in his day had spiritual needs. They were spiritually sick. They needed healing, salvation, and hope.

Military life certainly brings together people from a variety of backgrounds, but all of us have in common a need for Christ's mercy and salvation. Jesus prioritized people in need and gave them a place at his table.[28] Sisters, don't be afraid of different.

Respond

What have you learned about "different" since becoming a military wife? Differences abound, even among Christians. What challenges and opportunities are there when those differences are shared?

Prayer for the journey

Father, sometimes I don't like "different." It's more comfortable when people fit into my mold, especially when it comes to serving you. Help me find a deeper knowledge of you by focusing on what binds us together instead of what separates us. Amen.

Waypoint 13
Challenged or changed?

Read

> And when he was alone, those around him with the twelve asked him about the parables. And he said to them "To you has been given the secret of the kingdom of God, but for those outside everything is in parables, so that 'they may indeed see but not perceive, and may indeed hear but not understand, lest they should turn and be forgiven.' And he said to them, "Do you not understand this parable? How then will you understand all the parables?" (Mark 4:10–13)

Reflect

As Jesus traveled and taught many people heard his teaching and, just like many churchgoers today after hearing a good sermon, simply went home without understanding or turning their lives around.[29] Others, however, who heard Jesus teach and wanted to learn more. They hung around and listened as Jesus pulled the disciples aside for some intense leadership training and further explanation.[30]

Jesus had much to teach his twelve apostles to prepare them to carry on his mission after he was gone. They needed to know some secrets about the kingdom of God. They could not understand these secrets on their own. They needed the special revelation that only he could give. Aren't you encouraged to read that Jesus did not shoo away those who were not among the Twelve? He was willing to share the secrets with anyone who wanted to listen and learn.[31]

The situation is no different for us today. The only way we ever truly understand the Word of God is through the Holy Spirit who helps us. "When the Spirit of truth comes, he will guide you into all the truth" (John 16:3).

That is the reason you are encouraged to begin each daily Waypoint with the short prayer from Psalm 119:18: "Open my eyes, that I may behold wondrous things out of your law."

Jesus encountered those who admired his words, yet were content to watch from the periphery; and others who wanted to know more and pressed in closer to hear him elaborate on his teaching. The first group certainly included those challenged by Jesus' words. The second is where you would be more likely to find those who were changed by Jesus' truths. In which group would you be found?

Respond

Maybe you have read the Scriptures or a devotional entry and something seemed to jump off the page for you. How might that indicate Jesus taking you aside to help you understand his teaching? Are you standing on the periphery or pressing in to learn more about Jesus?

Prayer for the journey

Father, don't let me be content to stand on the periphery of truth. I don't want to just be challenged by your Word, I want to be changed. Give me a determination to press in and learn all you have to teach me. For your glory. Amen.

Waypoint 14

No need for a life preserver

> On that day, when evening had come, he said to them, "Let us go across to the other side." And leaving the crowd, they took him with them in the boat ... And a great windstorm arose, and the waves were breaking into the boat, so that the boat was already filling. But he was in the stern, asleep on the cushion. And they woke him and said to him, "Teacher, do you not care that we are perishing?" And he awoke and rebuked the wind and said to the sea, "Peace! Be still!" And the wind ceased, and there was a great calm. (Mark 4:35–39)

Reflect

As I type these words I watch a storm move across the ocean and spill onto the shore. The storm made a quick debut and the scene on the beach is anything but peaceful. The wind is blowing; people are frantic to pull down umbrellas and tents. And the beautiful morning had held such promise of a lazy day of beach-bum perfection.

Storms, literal or symbolic, can be swift and unexpected. But they are going to come. Even when you are serving Christ storms will come. The disciples would tell you storms come even when Jesus is right next to you.

The event described in Mark 4 was not your average storm. This storm threatened to overwhelm the boat with its furious wind. The disciples found themselves in a desperate situation and they were terrified. Don't miss the irony here: the carpenter, Jesus, was resting peacefully while the professional fishermen,

James, John, Andrew, and Peter, were frantic with fear.[32] Jesus was able to sleep because of his trust in God. The disciples did not see trust in his relaxation; they saw a lack of care and concern for their welfare.

Nothing was farther from the truth. Jesus was concerned enough for the disciples that he calmed the storm and gave them an "aha!" moment as they began to grasp who he really was (Mark 4:40–41). On a day when the disciples thought they would simply sail to the other side of the sea, they got a glimpse of the true identity of this one they followed. Only God had such power over nature. This storm became training ground for them to learn more of God's power.

There are days when my boat feels like it is capsizing. I share the anxiety expressed by poet e. e. cummings when he wrote, "King Christ, this world is all aleak;/and lifepreservers there are none."[33] Those are the days I remind myself I don't need a life preserver because Jesus is in the boat with me.

Respond

On a scale of one to ten, what is your response to storms of life, if one represents fear and ten represents faith?

Prayer for the journey

Lord, thank you that you are "a refuge and a shelter from the storm and rain" (Isaiah 4:6). Amen.

Waypoint 15

Laugh or serve?

> They came to the house of the ruler of the synagogue, and Jesus saw a commotion, people weeping and wailing loudly. And when he had entered, he said to them, "Why are you making a commotion and weeping? The child is not dead but sleeping." And they laughed at him. But he put them all outside and took the child's father and mother and those who were with him and went in where the child was. Taking her by the hand he said to her, "Talitha cumi," which means, "Little girl, I say to you, arise." And immediately the girl got up and began walking (for she was twelve years of age), and they were immediately overcome with amazement. And he strictly charged them that no one should know this, and told them to give her something to eat. (Mark 5:38–43)

Reflect

Here's a question for you: If you were there the day Jesus made the audacious claim, "The child is not dead but sleeping," would you be among those who laughed at him, or among those who would get up and give her something to eat when her life returned? Both?

Earlier in Mark 5, Jairus, the girl's father, went to find Jesus to plead with him to come and help his daughter, but Jesus was delayed and word came the daughter died. He had faith that Jesus could heal her, but now she was dead. All hope was gone. All faith was lost. She was not asleep. She was dead. The very presence of the mourners confirmed her demise.[34] Then this man Jesus made the foolhardy statement that she is not dead, only sleeping. Laughable.

Granted, laughter is a natural response to something that sounds outlandish. Laughter was ninety-year-old Sarah's response in Genesis 18:12 when God told her she would have a child in her old age. Her husband laughed as well when he received the same message. There was laughter of a different sort when their baby boy Isaac was born.

Back in the home of Jairus, Jesus touched the girl and she was no longer dead. He restored her to life. The laughter of unbelief surely turned to laughter of amazement in that place! Life needs nourishment, so Jesus commanded someone to give her something to eat. Oh, I hope I would be the one to jump up to get food to fill that girl's belly, laughing joyfully all the way to the kitchen!

Respond

Have you ever responded with laughter at something the Lord has asked of you? Has your laughter of skepticism ever been turned to the laughter of amazement at something the Lord has done?

Prayer for the journey

Lord, it is easy to laugh at things we find unbelievable. Your lavish love and unmerited grace are sometimes hard for me to believe. Forgive me when I laugh in disbelief that they can be mine. Amen.

Waypoint 16
Come away … and rest

Read

> The apostles returned to Jesus and told him all that they
> had done and taught. And he said to them, "Come away
> by yourselves to a desolate place and rest a while." For
> many were coming and going and they had no leisure
> even to eat. And they went away in the boat to a desolate
> place by themselves. (Mark 6:30–32)

Reflect

Do you ever get weary from doing good things? I sure do. I
wrote about my quest for rest one day in my journal:

> This morning I sit in silence. The banishment of the
> spoken word will not last all day, but for these few
> hours, the moratorium is self-imposed and necessary.
> For too many months, my days have held too much ac-
> tivity and too little reflection. (Yes, I inserted the word
> "too" on purpose *too many times* in that last sentence.)

> In the past few months, I have planned, prepared, pol-
> ished, and provided public presentations. (Obviously,
> lack of rest does not affect my use of alliteration.) I am
> tired. I know that relaxing my mind is important, but I
> tend to relax to the point of paralysis. True rest should
> provide inspiration and fresh creativity, but lately I've
> had nothin'. The well is dry.

Jesus knew about the need for rest in order to replenish the
soul. Pulling away for quiet moments was a part of his routine.
In Mark 6:30–31 we read of the disciples' return from a mission

trip. No doubt they were tired from their journey, but the needs of the crowds that came to see Jesus required so much attention they did not even have time to eat. In the midst of this commotion Jesus turned his attention on his disciples. They had been serving and caring for others and now they needed to experience care.[35] Jesus knew there was more service waiting for them, but the needs could wait a little while as they made a short boat ride across the river for a moment of rest.

I meet a lot of military wives who are beyond tired—they are weary. You may be among that number because of deployment, work, ministry, volunteering, family, chronic illness, or just the responsibilities of life. Will you notice the attention Jesus gives you today? Hear his voice say to you, "Come with me by yourselves to a quiet place and get some rest" (Mark 6:31b NIV).

Respond
What are the challenges you have in making time to rest? What can you do to make time for self-care?

Prayer for the journey
Lord, today I will be still before you and wait patiently for you (Psalm 37:7). Amen.

Waypoint 17

He sees the struggle

> And he saw that they were making headway painfully, for the wind was against them. And about the fourth watch of the night he came to them, walking on the sea. He meant to pass by them, but when they saw him walking on the sea they thought it was a ghost, and cried out, for they all saw him and were terrified. But immediately he spoke to them and said, "Take heart; it is I. Do not be afraid." (Mark 6:48–50)

Reflect

This morning I had a phone chat with a friend who lives in Seattle. She and her husband have taken up kayaking on the beautiful waters that surround that area. Most of the time they use individual kayaks and go out on a lake, but recently they decided to tandem kayak on Puget Sound. She described the lake waters as smooth and easy to maneuver. By contrast, rowing in the Sound was hard. They fought against the current in their attempt to row in sync and make headway. She said she could focus on nothing else but the struggle.

Struggles are like that, aren't they? My friend was struggling with water currents, but I could relate all she said to the struggles of life. It's easy to only focus on the struggle and thwart any forward movement. We move through the day with difficulty as if we are pushing against an emotional or situational current.

Just before today's Scripture passage, Jesus sent the disciples out into a boat to go ahead of him to the other side of the lake while he went off by himself to pray (Mark 6:45–52). Their encounter with the water was much like my friend described. They strained and struggled to make any headway in the challenging water.

Did you notice it was the Lord who sent them in the boat? In other words, they were in the Lord's will. Don't miss this: *A struggle does not mean you are out of the Lord's will.* We want relief from struggle, don't we? When it feels like there's no headway in ministry or spiritual growth, it feels like the Lord is far away, doesn't it?

Friends, the Lord sees us in our struggle. He saw the disciples and he came to them and spoke words of comfort and revelation, "Take heart; It is I. Do not be afraid."

Respond

What does this story reveal about the participation of Jesus in our struggles?

Prayer for the journey

Lord, help me not look so much for relief in the midst of struggle as to see you and your power working in my life. Amen.

Waypoint 18

A lifelong learner

Read

> And Jesus, aware of this, said to them, "Why are you discussing the fact that you have no bread? Do you not yet perceive or understand? Are your hearts hardened? Having eyes do you not see, and having ears do you not hear? And do you not remember?" (Mark 8:17–18)

Reflect

So far in their travels, the disciples have seen Jesus calm a horrific storm, heal diseased and infirmed people, and command demons to leave the possessed. They have seen Jesus raise a dead girl to life, walk on water, and feed thousands with a meager amount of food. They've heard teaching about the kingdom and have seen Jesus live that teaching through his words and actions. Yet here are the very same people—the ones closest to Christ, the ones we would consider religious experts—still unable to grasp the identity of Jesus. Talk about lack of perception! These men watched as he touched blind eyes and made them see, and deaf ears and made them hear and still could not see the truth of who he was nor hear the truth of what he taught.[36]

You may have heard the term "lifelong learning." It's something the military emphasizes as a way to open doors of opportunity. As a Christ follower you must commit yourself to lifelong learning about him. Sisters, with our best efforts we will never understand all there is to know about God and his work, but he will teach us more and more about him as we make ourselves open to his training.

Friend, there is no shame in not understanding the fullness of God. The only thing that must disappoint us is when we stop learning and think we've learned all there is to know. Or if, like the disciples, we forget what we've already learned.[37] We must be guided by the principle that the more we know him, the more we love him. The more we love him, the more we worship him. The more we worship him, the easier it is to trust his plan. The more we trust his plan, the more we want to be part of that plan.

Respond

I've known many long-time followers of Christ who have read through the Bible multiple times. Each time they say they understand things they did not understand before. Have you experienced this in your life yet? How?

Prayer for the journey

Lord, grant me a teachable spirit. Help me love you, know you, worship you, and live into your will. Amen.

Waypoint 19
Traveling and training

Read

> And Jesus went on with his disciples to the villages of Caesarea Philippi. And on the way he asked his disciples, "Who do people say that I am?" And they told him, "John the Baptist; and others say, Elijah; and others, one of the prophets." And he asked them, "But who do you say that I am?" Peter answered him, "You are the Christ." (Mark 8:27–29)

Reflect

I am one of those moms who takes full advantage of the captive audience that comes with a road trip. Yes, there is the perfunctory, "Are we there yet?" but that will not deter me from the mission at hand. What is the mission? On every trip, the inside of our vehicle becomes sacred space, a training ground, a place for impartation of faith, family, and fun into the lives of our kids.

Here in Mark, the road trip to Caesarea Philippi includes intense training with the twelve disciples. Teaching "on the way" was a strategy Jesus used with his disciples.[38] He took full advantage of the travel time to train them in kingdom principles. Today's Scripture illustrates that this was no occasion for chat or entertainment. The curriculum did not cover a minor issue. The lesson for this day was the most important question of all: Who is Jesus?

You may have noticed a recurring theme to this point in our journey with Jesus and his disciples: The disciples were a bit thick-headed. They did not get the meaning of Jesus' mission or the nature of their discipleship.[39]

The question Jesus asked is still one of the most discussed questions in the world. People still debate if he is just a prophet, just a teacher, just a religious man. Or is he more? Jesus brought the question home when he said, in essence, "Okay, I know what others say, but who do *you* say I am?" As spokesman for the group, Peter voices the uniqueness of Jesus as Messiah, God's promised Savior. At last, the truth about Jesus is recognized and acknowledged.[40]

The question is posed to you too, whether or not you have done extensive research on other religions and can explain what other people have said about Jesus. The most important answer any of us will ever have to give is our response to the Lord when he asks, "Who do you say I am?"

Respond

Who is Jesus to you? How has your view of Jesus changed as you have journeyed with him?

Prayer for the journey

Lord, things have not changed much over the centuries. Many people still appreciate you as a teacher and prophet, but they do not see you as Lord. Help me to proclaim the truth of who you are by my words and actions today. Give me the opportunity to share the story of my journey with you. Amen.

Waypoint 20

A mountaintop perspective

> And after six days Jesus took with him Peter and
> James and John, and led them up a high mountain by
> themselves. And he was transfigured before them,
> and his clothes became radiant, intensely white, as no
> one on earth could bleach them. And there appeared
> to them Elijah with Moses, and they were talking
> with Jesus. And Peter said to Jesus, "Rabbi, it is good
> that we are here. Let us make three tents, one for you
> and one for Moses and one for Elijah." For he did not
> know what to say, for they were terrified. And a cloud
> overshadowed them, and a voice came out of the cloud,
> "This is my beloved Son; listen to him." And suddenly,
> looking around, they no longer saw anyone with them
> but Jesus only. (Mark 9:2–8)

Reflect

Perspective has to do with the way objects appear or are
viewed. For instance, a realtor may use a wide-angle camera
to make a room look larger. Perspective can also be defined as
a mental view or outlook. Sometimes just placing myself in a
different environment gives me an improved perspective on my
circumstances.

Recently, I spent a week in the mountains of Colorado
with some military wives who are in the midst of deployment.
Mountain air, picturesque vistas, time to linger around the table,
deep and meaningful discussion all contributed to a refreshed
perspective of how to thrive in a less than optimum situation.

We left that mountain with renewed courage and energy to love and serve others.

One day Peter, James, and John spent some time on a mountain with Jesus. On that mountain their perspective on Jesus was changed. If they had any doubt of the identity of the one they had left everything to follow, those doubts were finally put to rest. (Can we all say together: It's about time!) How do you argue with clothes that become radiant before your eyes, a conversation with ancient prophets, and the voice of God using a cloud as a megaphone to endorse his Son?[41] This scriptural account of special effects is called the Transfiguration. The disciples witnessed a physical change in Jesus as he interacted with Moses, Elijah, and God the Father. They witnessed the glory of God, and it changed their perspective.

These disciples saw God as few on earth have. God did not use smoke and mirrors or the latest digital rendering, but through his miraculous power he revealed a small glimpse of Jesus' true glory. Whenever the Lord opens our eyes of faith to see a little more of him, we too come down the mountain not with only a new perspective on him, but as better people *for* him.

Respond
What is your perspective on Jesus now? Do you need to get off the trail and get alone with the Lord in order to gain a fresh view?

Prayer for the journey
Lord, give me eyes of faith to see more of your glory today. Amen.

Waypoint 21

Pass the salt

> "Salt is good, but if the salt has lost its saltiness, how will
> you make it salty again? Have salt in yourselves, and be
> at peace with one another." (Mark 9:50)

Reflect

The use of salt to preserve food used to be a necessity. The process can be traced back as far as Ancient Egypt. The most common techniques were dry-salting, in which meat or fish were buried in granular salt, or brine-curing, in which meat was soaked in strong salt water.[42]

Even the best techniques of preserving with salt can't compare with the preserving power found in the military MRE (Meals Ready to Eat). My Soldier husband still remembers the first time he ate food that was ten years old. To this day he is not sure it was a good idea to eat something with an unspecified shelf life.

The words found in Mark 9:50 are a small portion of the traveling training session Jesus had with his disciples on the road. The theme for that day's lesson could have been: "The Necessity of Salt." As disciples on mission for Christ, they were to influence society for good, just as salt is used to preserve and enhance the flavor of food.[43] Salt is recognized by its taste, and disciples who do not show the character of Christ are as useless as salt that has no flavor.[44]

Like salt preserving food in a hot climate, we want to preserve what is true and righteous in a decaying world.[45] That means standing up for what is right, promoting good causes, defending those who are weak and voiceless, helping those who cannot help themselves, and standing against those who would abuse and hurt others.

Salt also makes people thirsty. We want to make people thirsty for Christ by the way we show his love and forgiveness to one another. In Jesus' day, people also thought of salt as a symbol of wisdom or pleasing speech, critical for building good relationships.[46]

Jesus told his followers, "You are the salt of the earth" (Matthew 5:13). As Christ-followers we touch society, friends, and family with the goal of preserving all that is good and righteous. We don't do so with a stinging harshness, but with the wisdom of God, the compassion of Jesus, and healing words as prompted by the Holy Spirit.

Respond

How's your saltiness? Is there anything that keeps your life from making others thirsty? Are there relationships that need to be healed in order to carry out the Lord's instruction to be at peace with one another?

Prayer for the journey

Lord, don't let me lose my saltiness. Make me an agent of your preserving and healing power today. Amen.

Waypoint 22

One thing vs. everything

Read

> And as he was setting out on his journey, a man ran up and knelt before him and asked him, "Good Teacher, what must I do to inherit eternal life?" And Jesus said to him, "Why do you call me good? No one is good except God alone. You know the commandments: 'Do not murder, Do not commit adultery, Do not steal, Do not bear false witness, Do not defraud, Honor your father and mother.'" And he said to him, "Teacher, all these I have kept from my youth." And Jesus, looking at him, loved him, and said to him, "You lack one thing: go, sell all that you have and give to the poor, and you will have treasure in heaven; and come, follow me." Disheartened by the saying, he went away sorrowful, for he had great possessions. (Mark 10:17–22)

Reflect

The man who came to Jesus is someone we would consider "good." If he was in your military community, he would attend chapel and might serve as an usher. He would be squared away as a leader and would live his life by good and honorable principles. He would have a chest full of medals representing his wealth of experience over multiple deployments and years of sacrificial service to his nation. He looks forward to the day he will retire comfortably on his military pension. He comes to Jesus and asks what he has to do to have eternal life. Perhaps he is feeling a bit empty, even nervous. Surely there must be one more thing he can do to be certain.[47] Jesus tells him that to receive eternal life he must give up his medals, his service, and his military pension, and follow him. The man walks away grieving because his medals, his service, and his military benefits are his identity and his security.

What are you willing to give up to be a follower of Jesus? The rich man who approached Jesus thought maybe he just needed to add something to his already noble activities. He wanted Jesus to say "add this *one thing*," but instead Jesus said to give up *everything*.

Jesus does not make this direction to selling everything into a blanket requirement to following him, nor was he saying all his disciples must live in poverty. But the actions of Jesus emphasize that eternal life is not something we are able to obtain by virtue of our possessions, strength, wisdom, or authority. Dedication to Christ and his mission is not just something to add on to the other things that are important. The challenge of Jesus to those who would follow him is total commitment.[48]

Respond

Put yourself in the place of the person who approached Jesus. How would you respond to his requirement for achieving eternal life?

Prayer for the journey

Lord, help me count the cost of following you and empower me to serve you faithfully. Amen.

Waypoint 23

Leaders eat last

Read Mark 10:35-45

> And James and John, the sons of Zebedee, came up to him and said to him, "Teacher, we want you to do for us whatever we ask of you." And he said to them, "What do you want me to do for you?" And they said to him, "Grant us to sit, one at your right hand and one at your left, in your glory." (Mark 10:35–37)

Reflect

Leadership expert Simon Sinek was inspired to write a book he called *Leaders Eat Last*. The title was based on his conversation with a Marine Corps general. In an interview about the book, Sinek recalled asking the general, "What makes the Marine Corps so amazing?" The general responded with the three words, "Officers eat last." Sinek explains:

> If you go to a Marine Corps chow hall anywhere in the world, you will see the Marines lined up in rank order. The most senior person will be at the back of the line and the most junior person eats first. No one tells them they have to do it and it is not in any rulebook. It is because of the way they view the responsibility of leadership. We think leadership is about rank and power; they think of leadership as the responsibility for other human beings.[49]

Disciples and brothers James and John could have used some Marine Corps leadership training. Their self-centered request of Jesus was audacious and displayed their total lack of awareness concerning the mission of Jesus and those who would follow him. Once again, these guys weren't getting the message. This request comes directly on the heels of these words from Jesus: "But many who are first will be last, and the last first" (Mark 10:31). Jesus could not have been clearer that the role of his followers was to be the least of all and the servant of all.[50]

The request of James and John was not about service; it was about ambition and jealousy. They did not want to accomplish something—they wanted to be recognized. This request was about promoting themselves and not the Lord.

These disciples were handpicked by Jesus and here they were displaying selfish ambition, afraid one would get more recognition than the other. If we see this in the lives of the apostles who walked with Christ, don't be surprised if you see it in yourself or in other Christians. But Jesus' path to the head of the line is being the servant of all and responding to him in obedience.

Respond

Do you think there can be such a thing as godly ambition? If so, what might it look like?

Prayer for the journey

Lord, you came to serve, not to be served. You came to give and not receive. Purge me of selfish ambition and make me willing to serve others. Amen.

Waypoint 24

'We interrupt this journey ...'

Read

> And they came to Jericho. And as he was leaving Jericho with his disciples and a great crowd, Bartimaeus, a blind beggar, the son of Timaeus, was sitting by the roadside. And when he heard that it was Jesus of Nazareth, he began to cry out and say, "Jesus, Son of David, have mercy on me!" And many rebuked him, telling him to be silent. But he cried out all the more, "Son of David, have mercy on me!" And Jesus stopped and said, "Call him." And they called the blind man, saying to him, "Take heart. Get up; he is calling you." And throwing off his cloak, he sprang up and came to Jesus. And Jesus said to him, "What do you want me to do for you?" And the blind man said to him, "Rabbi, let me recover my sight." And Jesus said to him, "Go your way; your faith has made you well." And immediately he recovered his sight and followed him on the way. (Mark 10:46–52)

Reflect

My friend and fellow military wife Gwen has a great sign hanging on the wall of her kitchen. It reads, "Interruptions *are* my ministry." Is that how you view interruptions?

Military wives know something about interruptions, don't we? Military orders do not come with a courtesy call to find out if now is a convenient time. Some of the military interruptions I've experienced include:

- An interruption of a career
- An interruption of a holiday celebration

- An interruption of a school semester
- An interruption of a vacation
- An interruption while on a date with my husband ...

I could go on—as could you.

Have you noticed, as you read through the journeys of Jesus in the Gospel of Mark, how often he is interrupted? At least that is what it looks like from our perspective. This blind man sitting by the side of the road is one of many examples. Did Jesus really experience interruptions or was he just fulfilling his plan for his earthly ministry? Look at the way he responded to interruptions. There is no hint of annoyance or frustration about blind Bartimaeus breaking into his schedule. Instead, he met this interruption, like all the others, with compassionate service to whoever approached him.[51]

I have to ask myself: What if the interruptions in my life are opportunities to reach out to others and further mature me as a Christ follower?[52] Can God even use interruptions from the military to make that happen?

Respond

How would your view of military life change if you viewed the interruptions it brought as part of the mission of God for you? What opportunities might those interruptions hold?

Prayer for the journey

Lord, help me see any interruption as an opportunity for ministry today. Amen.

Waypoint 25

Don't go there!

> And they were on the road, going up to Jerusalem, and Jesus was walking ahead of them. And they were amazed, and those who followed were afraid. And taking the twelve again, he began to tell them what was to happen to him, saying, "See, we are going up to Jerusalem, and the Son of Man will be delivered over to the chief priests and the scribes, and they will condemn him to death and deliver him over to the Gentiles. And they will mock him and spit on him, and flog him and kill him. And after three days he will rise." (Mark 10:32–34).

Reflect

I remember when my husband's military orders arrived for Korea and I sighed, "Oh, no." I remember when my husband's military orders arrived for Ft. Bragg, and I sighed, "Oh, no." I remember when my husband's orders arrived for Washington, DC and I sighed, "Oh, no." You get the pattern. There were more times than not that military orders held destinations to which I did not want to go.

The account of Jesus in Mark 10:32–34 (moving back a few verses) amounts to him reading his upcoming "orders" to the disciples. His assignment in Jerusalem meant his death.

You can read about his celebratory arrival in Jerusalem in Mark 11:1–11. But even with the glowing reception Jesus first received there, it is safe to conclude Jerusalem was not a destination to which he looked forward. The Gospel of Luke tells us, "When the days drew near for him to be taken up, he set his face to go to Jerusalem" (Luke 9:51). I get the picture of him walking with purposeful and even urgent steps ahead of the disciples.[53] Jesus did not go to Jerusalem because he looked forward to suffering and dying on the cross. He went because he knew his sacrificial death would make possible eternal life for all who believe on him.

Sisters, as we travel on mission with God, we are sometimes asked to go where we do not want to go. Maybe it is possible that, at the place we don't want to go, the Lord has something he wants us to do.

When I look back at those places I did not want to go, I find that they hold some of my fondest memories. They were places of significant personal growth and meaningful service. Unlike Jesus, I could not see beforehand what my next destination held. But in retrospect, I give thanks to the Lord for the way he worked in my life in each assignment.

Respond
What have you learned from going to places you did not want to go? How do even those places fit into the mission God has for you? Are you in one of those places now?

Prayer for the journey
Show me the way I should go, for to you I entrust my life (Psalm 143:8b NIV).

Waypoint 26
Ambushed!

Read

And they came again to Jerusalem. And as he was walking in the temple, the chief priests and the scribes and the elders came to him, and they said to him, "By what authority are you doing these things, or who gave you this authority to do them?" Jesus said to them, "I will ask you one question; answer me, and I will tell you by what authority I do these things. Was the baptism of John from heaven or from man? Answer me." And they discussed it with one another, saying, "If we say, 'From heaven,' he will say, 'Why then did you not believe him?' But shall we say, 'From man'?"—they were afraid of the people, for they all held that John really was a prophet. So they answered Jesus, "We do not know." And Jesus said to them, "Neither will I tell you by what authority I do these things." (Mark 11:27–33)

Reflect

A popular morning show features a segment they call "Ambush Makeover." Beauty experts ambush an unsuspecting audience member, whisk her away and return her in an hour with updated hair, makeup, and clothes. The results are astounding. It's the kind of ambush I would welcome.

There are other times when an ambush is not so welcome. Christ-followers get ambushed all the time, don't we? For instance, how many times have you been ambushed with questions like, "Why would a loving God allow war? Suffering?

Disappointment?" Sometimes people are genuinely looking for an answer, but often the questions are asked in a sarcastic tone.

Jesus was ambushed by the religious leaders of his day with the question, "By what authority are you doing these things?" The question was not asked from any desire to learn the truth, but to catch Jesus off guard in a "wrestle for control."[54] They confronted Jesus as if they were conducting an interrogation. The setting does not convey an open-minded request for information.[55]

Certainly Jesus could win any argument, but he was not argumentative here. He used the techniques of the rabbis better than they did! He offered to answer their question. But first he asked them to validate their authority to question his authority by answering a question he posed.[56] His response defused the confrontation because the leaders no longer wanted to proceed with the argument. They are left uttering the words, "we don't know …" Sisters, there is a lesson here for us: There is a time to argue the facts and a time to realize that arguments will not produce anything good.

Respond

How do you respond when you are ambushed with questions about your faith? How can you defuse such confrontations?

Prayer for the journey

Lord, help me always be prepared to make a defense with gentleness and respect to anyone who asks me for a reason for the hope that is in me (1 Peter 3:15). Amen.

Waypoint 27
What's your METL?

> And one of the scribes came up and heard them disputing with one another, and seeing that he answered them well, asked him, "Which commandment is the most important of all?" Jesus answered, "The most important is, 'Hear, O Israel: The Lord our God, the Lord is one. And you shall love the Lord your God with all your heart and with all your soul and with all your mind and with all your strength.' The second is this: 'You shall love your neighbor as yourself.' There is no other commandment greater than these." (Mark 12:28–31)

Reflect

Among the plethora of military acronyms is METL: Mission Essential Task List. Simply put, METL is a list of things that are nonnegotiable to accomplish a mission.

If we read Mark 12:28–31 with military mission in mind, we could say it includes the METL for a Christ-follower. First on the list: Love the Lord. Second on the list: Love your neighbor. Sisters, our METL is held in these two sentences.

Put yourself in the place of the scribe questioning Jesus. "Which commandment is the most important of all?" He was not expecting a simple answer. He knew there are 365 prohibitions and 248 positive commands in the Torah or Jewish Law.[57] But the answer Jesus gives was both succinct and compelling.

Jesus's words emphasize too that following him is not about a list of things we must do for God's approval. Following

Jesus is a call to himself. It is a call to love him supremely and to love others as we love ourselves. Loving others is the visible expression and practical display of my love for God. It is how God's love spills over in my life.

At first, it would seem that Jesus made serving God easier by narrowing the list of commands from 613 to two. But when followed wholeheartedly, these two commands inspire an unlimited number of actions. The METL of a military unit is usually short and simple to read, but it can can be complex and challenging to accomplish, and must be continuously practiced. The METL Jesus provides for our lives is short and easy to memorize, but we never can check off the list as complete. We make every effort, by faith in Christ, to increase our love for God and others.

Respond

What have you done over the last week to support these two primary tasks in life?

Prayer for the journey

Lord, show me the things that keep me from loving you with my whole heart. Increase my love for you, and show me ways to demonstrate that love in my love of others. Amen.

Waypoint 28

Two coins

> And he sat down opposite the treasury and watched the people putting money into the offering box. Many rich people put in large sums. And a poor widow came and put in two small copper coins, which make a penny. And he called his disciples to him and said to them, "Truly, I say to you, this poor widow has put in more than all those who are contributing to the offering box. For they all contributed out of their abundance, but she out of her poverty has put in everything she had, all she had to live on." (Mark 12:41–44)

Reflect

Small. Minimal. Insignificant. Trivial. Unimportant. Irrelevant. Inconsequential.

These words may have been in her mind as the poor widow dropped the coins into the offering box. What the woman contributed was the smallest denomination of currency in use at the time.[58] Each coin was less than a penny. The gift quite possibly left her without the means for her next meal.[59] Her generosity is an example for us to follow. She could have given just one of the coins, but she was down to her last penny and she gave it all.

Huge. Maximum. Significant. Monumental. Important. Relevant. Useful.

These words point to the way Jesus viewed the widow's action. Notice that Jesus sat down opposite the offering box. He stopped. He rested. He observed what people were doing and he noticed this poor widow.

Let the beauty of this scene wash over you. Maybe words like small, minimal, insignificant, trivial, unimportant, irrelevant, and inconsequential describe how you feel about what you have to offer God. But God does not judge you by your own standards, nor the standards of the world. He is observing what you are able to give, and his system of evaluation is different than our system. The giver matters more to him than the gift.

He noticed the poor widow's heart, not what the gift could buy. He notices you, my sister, and he values whatever you give to him and to others in his name.

Respond

Does anything make you feel like what you have to offer God is not enough? Grab your journal and jot down God's truth about you and your offering from these Scriptures:

- Galatians 2:20
- Isaiah 43:1
- 1 Peter 2:9

Prayer for the journey

Lord, remind me that your eye watches over those who fear you and rely on your unfailing love (Psalm 33:18). Amen.

Waypoint 29
She did what she could

And while he was at Bethany in the house of Simon the leper, as he was reclining at table, a woman came with an alabaster flask of ointment of pure nard, very costly, and she broke the flask and poured it over his head. There were some who said to themselves indignantly, "Why was the ointment wasted like that? For this ointment could have been sold for more than three hundred denarii and given to the poor." And they scolded her.

But Jesus said, "Leave her alone. Why do you trouble her? She has done a beautiful thing to me. For you always have the poor with you, and whenever you want, you can do good for them. But you will not always have me. She has done what she could; she has anointed my body beforehand for burial. And truly, I say to you, wherever the gospel is proclaimed in the whole world, what she has done will be told in memory of her." (Mark 14:3–9)

Reflect

At face value it is hard to grasp the custom, but in Jesus' day it was common for olive oil to be poured on the heads of guests as a symbol of honor and a rite of refreshment. The oil was soothing to dry, parched skin. In Mark 14:3–9 Jesus was at a dinner party with friends and a woman entered the room carrying a jar filled not even with common oil but with expensive perfume. She broke the jar and drenched Jesus with it. Her action was as extravagant as the contents of the jar.

The onlookers, perhaps concerned to look good before the rabbi were quick to scold the woman. They saw her excessive offering as a waste of valuable resources. Jesus stopped their attack, and then he said these words: "She has done what she could."

Think about those words. "She did what she could."

A doctor says "I did what I could" when a patient dies.

A parent says "I did what I could" when a child goes astray.

I say "I did what I could" when I need an excuse for not doing my best.

"I did what I could" is a phrase of resignation when I am not able to do what needs to be done, when I can only do a portion of an assignment. I say those words when I cannot do enough.

When Jesus uttered that phrase it was not to criticize the woman for not doing enough. To the contrary, she did exactly what she needed to do.

The Spirit of God was orchestrating every event of the week that led to the death and resurrection of Jesus. The Spirit motivated this woman to serve Jesus in an extravagant manner. Jesus saw it as anointing him for burial, pointing to his imminent crucifixion. That's why the memory of her act is associated with the proclamation of the gospel.

When you put all you can do in the hands of the Lord, he can make it *more than enough.*

Respond

What are some words that come to mind when you think of the woman's actions toward Jesus? What words describe your actions toward Jesus this week?

Prayer for the journey

Lord, give me a sensitive and sacrificial heart toward you in gratitude for all you have done for me. Amen.

Waypoint 30
A Bystander

Read

> And they compelled a passerby, Simon of Cyrene, who
> was coming in from the country, the father of Alexander
> and Rufus, to carry his cross. (Mark 15:21)

Reflect

The last journey of Jesus before his death was to walk a road we
now call his Via Dolorosa—the Way of Sorrows. It was the final
segment of the most important journey ever taken.

If you go to Jerusalem today you can walk the Via Dolorosa.
The route passes through congested streets replete with snack
stands and souvenir shops. Historians differ on the exact route
Jesus took on his way to the cross, but pilgrims still find great
significance in being in close proximity to his path. Each Friday
afternoon a Catholic priest leads a procession that repeats the
final journey of Jesus from the Praetorium of Pilate to the hill of
Golgotha, site of the crucifixion.[60]

The final road Jesus walked was one no human could
survive. He knew it meant death. His body became weak as he
struggled to carry the weight of his cross. The custom of the day
allowed Roman soldiers to commandeer local citizens to carry
excess baggage for them. On this day the soldiers interrupted
the life of a bystander, Simon of Cyrene, to carry the cross for
the condemned Jesus.

There is no question that Simon was forced to bear the cross
for Christ, but I also see the situation as him being invited by
God to participate in this most important mission. People were
called to participate in the mission of Jesus from his birth to his

death and resurrection. Such was the case for Simon. He was not a simple bystander. He walked the road. He carried the burden.

Simon could represent each one of us. We are not forced, but we are called to bear the cross of Christ. For a few minutes, the cross of Christ became Simon's cross to bear.

There is a cost to be identified with Jesus. There is also joy in walking beside him. The joy for Simon most likely included becoming a follower of Christ. Numerous biblical scholars believe Simon became a dedicated believer, and that his sons Alexander and Rufus became leaders in the early Christian church.[61]

The cross represents the mission of Christ. Jesus used the same metaphor to describe his mission for us when he said, "Whoever wants to be my disciple must deny themselves and take up their cross and follow me" (Mark 8:34 NIV). What mission does Christ have for you? What road does he have for you to walk? Just as Simon walked beside Jesus, you can rest assured that Jesus will walk beside you.

Respond

What does it mean to you to "deny yourself and take up your cross?"

Prayer for the journey

Lord, thank you for inviting me to be part of your mission in the world. Let your will be my will. Amen.

Notes for Journey 1

1.   Betty Sowers and Bonnie Stone, *Campfollowing: A History of the Military Wife* (Westport, CT: Praeger, 1991), 14.

2.   God changed the names Abram and Sarai to Abraham and Sarah later on the journey. Abraham and Sarah will be used throughout this series.

3.   John H. Walton, *The NIV Application Commentary: Genesis* (Grand Rapids, MI: Zondervan, 2001), 392.

4.   Allen P. Ross, *Creation & Blessing, A Guide to the Study and Exposition of Genesis* (Grand Rapids, MI: Baker Book House, 1988), 263.

5.   Bill T. Arnold, *Encountering the Book of Genesis* (Grand Rapids, MI: Baker Books, 2003), 72.

6.   Walter Brueggemann, "Placed between Promise and Command," in *Rooted in the Land, Essays on Community and Place,*" eds. William Vitek & Wes Jackson (New Haven, CT: Yale University Press, 1996), 124.

7.   W. Lee Humphreys, *The Character of God in the Book of Genesis* (Louisville, KY: Westminster John Knox Press, 2001), 85.

8.   Claus Westermann, *Continental Commentary, Genesis 12-36* (Minneapolis: Augsburg Publishing House, 1995), 155.

9.   Walton, 398.

10. Ibid., 396.

11. Walter Bruggemann, *Genesis* (Atlanta: John Knox Press, 1982), 126.

12. R. Kent Huges, *Genesis: Beginning and Blessing* (Wheaton, IL: Crossway, 2004), 196.

13. Humphries, 87.

14. Walton, 424.

15. Westermann, 181.

16. Ibid, 177.

17. Bob Deffenbaugh, "Lot Looks Out for Number One (Genesis 13:5-18)." https://bible.org/seriespage/lot-looks-out-number-one-genesis-135-18 (accessed January 5, 2014).

18. Westermann, 180.

19. Anthony Bell, "Family Readiness Group Grows Through Leadership, Selfless Service," *Fort Lee Traveler,* December 5, 2013, http://www.ftleetraveller.com/news/local_news/article_a224effe-5d2b-11e3-87d0-0019bb2963f4.html (accessed February 2, 2014).

20. Bruce Waltke, *Genesis: A Commentary* (Grand Rapids, MI: Zondervan, 2001), 249.

21. Westermann, 311.

22. Waltke, 259

23. Ibid.

24. Westermann, 260.

25. *Paul Borgman, Genesis: The Story We Haven't Heard* (Downers Grove, IL: InterVarsity Press, 2001), B60.

26. Bill Arnold, *Encountering the Book of Genesis* (Grand Rapids, MI: Baker Publishing Group, 2003), 97.

27. Arnold, 101.

28. Ibid, 102.

29. Ibid, 100.

30. Waltke, 272.

31. Walton, 470.

32. Arnold, 102.

33. Waltke, 300.

34. Waltke, 292.

35. Westermann, 332.

36. Walton, 518.

37. Waltke 322.

38. Gerhard von Rad, *Genesis: A Commentary.* (Philadelphia: Westminister John Knox Press, 1972), 250.

39. Borgman, 38.

40. Walton, 402.

41. Karen Jowers, "Suvey: More Spouses Satisfied with Army Life." http://www.armytimes.com/article/20110307/NEWS/103070335/Survey-More-spouses-satisfied-Army-life (accessed February 21, 2014).

Notes for Journey 2

1. John Tierney "Good News Beats Bad on Social Networks," *New York Times*, March 18, 2013, accessed August 24, 2014, http://www.nytimes.com/2013/03/19/science/good-news-spreads-faster-on-twitter-and-facebook.html?pagewanted=all&_r=0.

2. Francis J. Moloney, *The Gospel of Mark* (Grand Rapids: Baker Academic, 2012), 31.

3. Bob Deffinbaugh, "The Call of Abram," www.bible.org, accessed July 26, 2014, https://bible.org/seriespage/call-abram-genesis-1131-199.

4. "Rosie the Riveter." www.History.com, accessed August 8, 2014. http://www.history.com/topics/world-war-ii/rosie-the-riveter.

5. R. T. France, *The New International Greek Testament Commentary: The Gospel of Mark* (Grand Rapids: Wm. B. Eerdmans Publishing Co. 2002), 77–78.

6. William L. Lane, *The New International Commentary of the New Testament: The Gospel of Mark* (Grand Rapids: Wm. B. Eerdmans Publishing Co., 1974), 57.

7. David E. Garland, *Zondervan Illustrated Bible Background Commentary: Mark* (Grand Rapids: Zondervan, 2007), 9.

8. France, 85.

9. See also Matthew 4:1–11 and Luke 4:1–13.

10. France, 94.

11. Bonnie B. Thurston, *Preaching Mark* (Minneapolis: Fortress Press: Minneapolis, 2002), 18.

12. France, 90.

13. Anne Voscamp, "When You Ache with Ordinary Life," A Holy Experience, August 30, 2010, accessed August 9, 2014, shttp://www.aholyexperience.com/2010/08/when-you-ache-with-ordinary-life.

14. Moloney, 53.

15. Lane, 69.

16. France, 95.

17. Lt. Col. Daniel Gernert, "Why do we serve in the military?" Air Education and Training Command Commentary, accessed July 29, 2014, www.aetc.af.mil/news/story.asp?id=123-26914.

18. Garland, 14.

19. David E. Garland, *The NIV Application Commentary: Mark* (Grand Rapids, MI: Zondervan, 1996), 72.

20. Ray B. Williams, "Early Risers Are Happier, Healthier and More Productive than Night Owls," *Psychology Today*, August 20, 2012, accessed July 29, 2014. http://www.psychologytoday.com/blog/wired-success/201208/early-risers-are-happier-healthier-and-more-productive-night-owls.

21. France, 101.

22. R. Kent Hughes, *Mark: Jesus, Servant and Savior, Volume 1* (Westchester, IL: Crossway Books, 1989), 49.

23. Marie Hobson, "Military Wives Are Anything But Dependent," *The Moderate Voice*, accessed July 30, 2014. http://themoderatevoice. com/110408/military-spouses-are-anything-but-dependent.

24. France, 124.

25. N. T. Wright, *Mark for Everyone* (Louisville: Westminster John Knox Press, 2004), 20.

26. Morna D. Hooker, *The Gospel According to Saint Mark: Black's New Testament Commentary* (Grand Rapids: Baker Academic, 2009), 96.

27. France, 134.

28. Ibid.

29. France, 194.

30. Ibid.

31. Hooker, 126.

32. Garland, 191.

33. Quoted in Garland, 199.

34. France, 239.

35. France, 264.

36. Moloney, 161.

37. Hooker, 196.

38. France, 326.

39. Hooker, 200.

40. France, 330.

41. France, 348.

42. "Food Preservation," www.Tudorhistory.org, accessed July 13, 2014. http://tudorhistory.org/topics/food/preserve.html.

43. France, 384.

44. Hooker, 233.

45. Hughes, 42.

46. France, 385.

47. Moloney, 199.

48. Hooker, 242.

49. Dan Schawbel, "Why Leaders Should Always Eat Last, Simon Sinek Interview," *The Fast Track*, February 19, 2014, accessed July 14, 2014. http://quickbase.intuit.com/blog/2014/02/19/why-leaders-should-always-eat-last-simon-sinek-interview.

50. Moloney, 192.

51. Frances Taylor Gench, *Back to the Well: Women's Encounters with Jesus in the Gospels* (Louisville: Westminster John Knox Press, 2004), 52.

52. Thurston, 66–67.

53. France, 411.

54. Craig A. Evans, *Word Biblical Commentary: Mark 8:27–16:20* (Nashville: Thomas Nelson, 2001), 198.

55. France, 452.

56. Evans, 205.

57. Hooker, 288.

58. France, 493.

59. Ibid.

60. Bargil Pixner, *Paths of the Messiah and Sites of the Early Church from Galilee to Jerusalem* (San Francisco: Ignatius Press, 2010), 303.

61. Ibid, 641.

Thank you for coming along with Brenda on this encounter with God's Word!

We pray that God will continue to encourage you in the next season of your life. To continue your journey in Scripture, look for the other books in this series:

- **Dedicated: Steps of Faith in God's plan**

- **Devoted: Steps of Love Toward Healthy Relationships**

- **Deployed: Steps of Hope in Times of Uncertainty**

- **Directed: Steps of Peace in Times of Transition**

You can find them, along with other small group materials and resources to start your own online community at **www.MilitaryWife.bible.**

You can also order free copies of these books for other military wives at **ArmedServicesMinistry.com.**

We need your help... How has God's Word impacted your life?

Dear Military Wife,

American Bible Society is honored to share this Journey with you! Thank you for your selfless devotion to your husband and our country.

Generous contributions from our supporters make it possible for us to provide these resources to you free of charge. As a way of thanking these faithful supporters, we love to share stories of how our Scripture resources have made a difference in someone's life.

Please take a moment to fill out the postage-paid card to the right and share how this Journey has impacted your life.

You may provide us with your name or remain anonymous.

Thank you and God bless you!

Annie LoCastro
Armed Services Ministry Program Manager
Email: **Provisions@AmericanBible.org**

Check out our website for other devotions:
www.MilitaryWife.bible

JOURNEY OF A MILITARY WIFE: DEDICATED

In what branch of service does (or did) your husband serve?

Check current status:
☐ **ACTIVE DUTY** ☐ **RESERVES/NATIONAL GUARD** ☐ **VETERAN**

This Journey has positively influenced my perception of the Bible and its message for me and my family.
☐ **YES** ☐ **NO**

Did this Journey encourage you to further explore the Bible and God's promises?
☐ **YES** ☐ **NO**

Did you read through this Journey as part of a group or study?
☐ **YES** ☐ **NO**

How has this Journey helped you better apply the Bible to your life? What positive action did you take?

_____

_____

_____

_____

☐ Please send me another Bible Study. Here is my name and email address.

_____
NAME

_____
EMAIL

☐ **YES** ☐ **NO**
I would like someone from the American Bible Society to contact me so I can share my story and how this Bible has impacted my life. *Someone will* **ONLY** *contact you* **if** *the Yes space is checked.*

124538